Disinvestment of Foreign Subsidiaries

Research for Business Decisions, No. 25

Gunter Dufey, Series Editor
Professor of International Business and Finance
The University of Michigan

Other Titles in This Series

No. 18 Decision Making in Multinational Corporations   Donna G. Goehle

*No. 19 The Changing Labor Content of American
Foreign Trade, 1970-1975*   John A. Kilpatrick

*No. 20 Currency Translation and Performance
Evaluation in Multinationals*   Helen Gernon Morsicato

*No. 21 Organization of Information Services:
A Contingency Approach*   Margrethe H. Olson

*No. 22 Penetrating the U.S. Auto Market:
German and Japanese Strategies, 1965-1976*   James Rader

No. 23 Decision Making in Continuous Steel Casting   Mark A. Vonderembse

*No. 24 Management Career Progress in
a Japanese Organization*   Mitsuru Wakabayashi

Disinvestment of Foreign Subsidiaries

by
Brent D. Wilson

umi
RESEARCH PRESS

Produced and distributed by
UMI Research Press
an imprint of
University Microfilms International
Ann Arbor, Michigan 48106

Library of Congress Cataloging in Publication Data

Wilson, Brent D   1944-
   Disinvestment of foreign subsidiaries.

   (Research for business decisions ; no. 25)
   Bibliography: p.
   Includes index.
   1. Investments, American. 2. Corporations, American.
I. Title. II. Series.
HG4538.W444   338.8'8973   80-18601
ISBN 0-8357-1132-3

Contents

Figures and Tables   vii

1 Introduction to Foreign Disinvestment   1

2 Foreign Investment Theories   13

3 Economic Evaluation of a Disinvestment   21

4 Tests of the Disinvestment Model   33

5 The Role of Facilitating Factors in Disinvestment   49

6 Disinvestment Case Studies   63

7 Summary   71

   Notes   81

   Appendix A: The Logistic Regression Model   85

   Bibliography   87

   Index   89

Figures and Tables

Figures

1-1   Growth in Number of Foreign Subsidiaries of 180 U.S. Based
Multinational Enterprises, 1951-1975 3

1-2   Growth in Number of Foreign Manufacturing Subsidiaries
of 180 U.S. Based Multinational Enterprises, 1951-1975............ 4

1-3   Number of Foreign Subsidiaries of 180 U.S. Based
Multinational Enterprises Exiting from Systems
(Excluding Mergers), 1951-1975 5

Tables

1-1   Method of Exit 6

3-1   Hypothesized Impact of Disinvestment Model 31

4-1   Summary of Logistic Regression Equations 47

5-1   Correlation Matrix 54

5-2   Logistic Regressions for Change in Chief Executive Officer (CEO) 55

5-3   Logistic Regressions for Change in
Chief Operating Officer (COO) 57

5-4   Logistic Regressions for Decrease in System Net Income (NI) 58

5-5   Logistic Regressions for Best Individual Variables 59

5-6   Multiple Logistic Regression for All Variables 60

7-1   Summary of Results of Tests of Hypothesis 74

7-2   Comparison of Results with Caves and Porter
Study of Disinvestments 76

1

Introduction to Foreign Disinvestment

As U.S. corporations have grown, the scope of their operations has expanded to include foreign markets. This broadening of horizons has fostered the term "multinational" to describe their nature. The multinational aspect of these large corporations has been amply demonstrated by various studies. These studies have shown that many U.S. multinationals derive significant percentages of their sales and profits outside of the United States.[1]

To provide for this expansion in foreign sales, U.S. multinational companies have expanded the number of foreign subsidiaries. The Harvard Multinational Enterprise study has documented the foreign development of the 180 largest U.S. based multinational companies through 1975.[2] By the end of 1975, these multinationals had over 11,000 subsidiaries.[3]

However, even as the number of subsidiaries of these multinationals has grown, another activity has also occurred: the disinvestment of existing subsidiaries. In view of the increasing importance of foreign markets to U.S. multinationals and the phenomenal growth in foreign subsidiaries, it seems incongruous that disinvestments should be occurring. One would expect that, if disinvestments should occur, it would be on a small scale that could be explained as "error corrections."

Nevertheless, evidence of the magnitude of disinvestments by U.S. multinational companies is beginning to be assembled, and it indicates that adjustment for management mistakes is not a sufficient explanation. The purpose of this study is to develop a model of disinvestment activity. It will attempt to answer the questions of why and when disinvestment occurs.

Prior to attempting to develop a model to explain the disinvestment activity, it is important to examine the scope of disinvestments. After this examination, a review of previous studies of disinvestment will be undertaken to provide a base for this study.

I. The Scope of Foreign Disinvestment

The Harvard Multinational Enterprise study, which includes data on the subsidiaries of the 180 largest U.S. based multinational companies, provides some useful information in determining the magnitude and importance of disinvestment of foreign subsidiaries. As noted above, these multinationals accounted for over 11,000 foreign subsidiaries by 1975. This study also traces the development of these subsidiaries from 1900 through 1975. An analysis of this data base provides some pertinent information in regard to disinvestment of foreign subsidiaries.

Beginning in 1950, the number of subsidiaries which exited from the parent system was about 25 annually. This number does not include those subsidiaries which exited through mergers. The annual number of exits increased during the early 1960s to a high of 329 in 1967. Since that peak, the number has remained relatively constant at about 260 annually.

Figure 1-1 illustrates the growth in new subsidiaries and the increase in the number of exits from existing subsidiaries (excluding subsidiaries which exited through mergers). The peak annual net growth occurred in 1968 when the stock of subsidiaries was increased by 774. This increase has steadily diminished since that point to a level of 109 in 1975. The ratio of new subsidiaries to exits has declined from 10.2:1 during 1961-5 to 1.4:1 in 1975.[4]

An examination of the manufacturing subsidiaries alone yields similar results. Figure 1-2 shows a similar pattern to Figure 1-1, which included all subsidiaries.

Although the rate of increase in new subsidiaries has slowed, the number of exits has not fallen proportionally. This differing pattern indicates that different factors may be affecting these developments. One possibility is that an increase in governmental expropriations of subsidiaries has offset a reduction in exits due to other factors. Certainly expropriations are well reported in the media and gain much attention; however, the increase in expropriations does not seem to entirely explain the exit phenomenon. Figure 1-3 compares the number of exits through expropriations to the total number of exits. This shows that expropriations have not increased significantly in their share of total exits. Although the number of expropriations has increased over the years to a high of 42 in 1975, the number of subsidiaries sold or liquidated has also been increasing as shown in Table 1-1.

Although part of the explanation for the disinvestment activity may be found in expropriations, there are obviously other factors at work. The identification of these other factors is the purpose of this study.

II. Previous Studies of Disinvestment

As noted in the examination of the magnitude of foreign disinvestment, it has only been in recent years that disinvestment of foreign subsidiaries has taken on significant proportions. However, disinvestment of domestic subsidiaries has received attention for some time. As a result, most of the studies of disinvestment have focused on domestic subsidiaries rather than on foreign.

Figure 1-1

**Growth in Number of Foreign Subsidiaries of 180
U.S. Based Multinational Enterprises, 1951-1975**

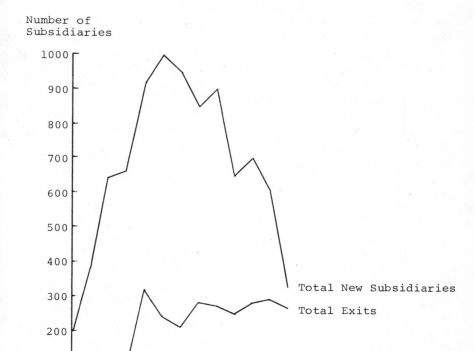

* Average for the period

Source: Harvard Multinational Enterprise Study

Figure 1-2

**Growth in Number of Foreign Manufacturing Subsidiaries of 180
U.S. Based Multinational Enterprises, 1951-1975**

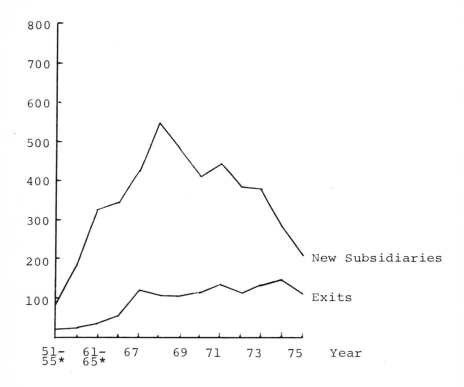

Number of
Subsidiaries

* Average for the period

Source: Harvard Multinational Enterprise Study

Figure 1-3

**Number of Foreign Subsidiaries of 180
U.S. Based Multinational Enterprises Exiting from Systems
(Excluding Mergers), 1951-1975**

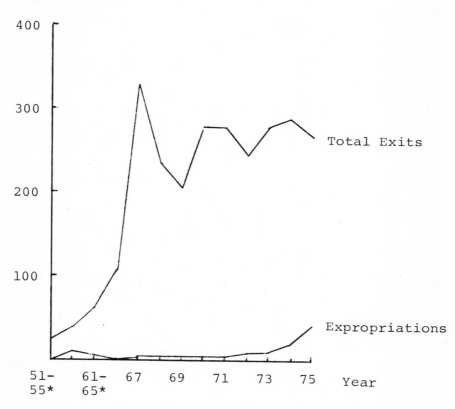

* Average for the period

Source: Harvard Multinational Enterprise Study

Table 1-1

Method of Exit of Foreign Subsidiaries of 180 U.S. Based Multinational Enterprises, 1951-1975

Method of Exit	51-55	56-60	61-65	66	67	68	69	70	71	72	73	74	75	51-75
Sold	40	47	82	41	167	110	125	171	146	148	147	158	133	1515
Liquidated	52	80	157	60	151	117	78	103	124	89	124	112	92	1339
Expropriated	1	54	24	0	3	2	3	2	3	8	9	18	42	169
Unknown	23	26	53	8	8	3	1	1	1	3	0	2	0	129
TOTAL	116	207	316	109	329	232	207	277	274	248	280	290	267	3152

Source: Curhan, et al., *Tracing the Multinationals*, p. 165.

Thus, it will be necessary to extrapolate the conclusions of the domestic studies into the multinational environment.

Studies of Domestic Disinvestment

Most of the early work in the area of disinvestment focused on the problems of "how to do it." Hillman and Soden suggested that disinvestment should be an integral part of a company's strategy.[5] They explained that a proper strategic approach to disinvestment would facilitate the marketing of the subsidiary. They seemed to believe that the marketing of the subsidiary was the primary problem in disinvestment.

Wallender also took a planning approach to the problem.[6] However, he suggested some reasons why corporations did not plan for disinvestments:

1. Disinvestment is final with no alternatives as in growth by acquisition or expansion.
2. Disinvestment is contrary to the basic motives of corporate staff and is avoided at almost all levels of planning.
3. Disinvestment is usually linked with failure and it tends to be accompanied by morale problems.
4. Disinvestment can have serious repercussions on the image of the corporation or the unit divested.
5. Disinvestment activities require expertise which should be obtained from specialists rather than from other executives who should not be taken away from their normal activities.[7]

He then outlined methods by which the planning for disinvestment could be improved. These included early identification of candidates for disinvestment followed by actions to facilitate the disinvestment. Other suggestions focused on the attitudinal problems of disinvestment. He stressed that through a planning program, executives will recognize that disinvestment is an element of a dynamic company rather than a symbol of failure.

Gilmour studied in detail three cases of disinvestment.[8] Based on these situations, he suggested that disinvestment decisions are made too late and are based on little hard data. He concluded that the nature of the decision could be summarized as follows:

1. Disinvestment decisions are difficult.
2. Disinvestment requires admission of failure by a key manager. These are not necessarily "bad managers."
3. Analysis for the disinvestment was done after the decision had been made. As a result, other alternatives were not analyzed.
4. The decisions were made at the highest level in the organization.

In addition, he noted that the decisions were made by new management which did not have the biases or loyalties of previous management and could make the disinvestment decisions without losing face.

His model of disinvestment suggests that disinvestment occurs when there is a discrepancy between personal or organizational goals and the situation facing the company. Disinvestment decisions are not recognition of future states, but rather come about as reactions to problems which exist. Whether a disinvestment is made depends on the personal commitment and persuasiveness of committed managers.

The primary focus of these studies was the process of disinvestment. They examined how subsidiaries are disinvested without reviewing the factors leading to the decisions to disinvest. As such, they do not answer the basic questions of this study: why and when does disinvestment occur?

A study by Caves and Porter sheds some light on these questions.[9] They hypothesized that disinvestment would occur when a subsidiary has a low return on investment, this low return has existed for a period of time, and the products are considered mature. Given these conditions, they then attempted to determine what factors would prevent a firm from disinvesting a subsidiary. These factors were termed "barriers to exit." They suggested that barriers to exit exist because some of the inputs to the subsidiary are durable and specific to the activity of that subsidiary. These durable and specific assets (DSAs) were grouped into three general categories: tangible and intangible fixed assets, joint production, and managerial behavior.

Tangible fixed assets which are considered DSAs are assets which are long-lived and have little value outside the subsidiary. Examples are specialized equipment and work in process and finished goods inventories. Intangible DSAs are assets such as trademarks and franchising arrangements. Because of the potential high cost of terminating labor in a liquidation situation, it might be considered in this category. The important aspect of these assets is that they have less value to another company than to the company currently employing them.

Joint production assets refer to those which are linked to other aspects of the company's overall operations. These assets might be shared production facilities or distribution systems. If a particular subsidiary was producing products complementary to others in the system or was part of a vertically integrated organization, these factors would be considered another type of asset.

Management may also develop specific skills which are of less value to other companies. In addition, management may have developed loyalty to particular subsidiaries, or be unwilling to terminate workers. Another barrier for management is the aura of failure which typically surrounds a disinvestment.

The result of these barriers is that companies do not disinvest when, according to the original hypothesis, it would be economically justified.

In a further refinement of this model, Porter reclassified the entry barriers into structural or economic (tangible and intangible fixed assets), corporate strategy (joint production), and managerial (managerial behavior).[10] He also stressed the role of the managerial barriers as being very critical. In his exposition of the managerial barriers, he segmented them into two categories: information-related and conflicting goals.

Information-related barriers exist when management does not have the necessary information to make disinvestment decisions. This situation is most likely to occur in cases where financial data is not compiled for each unit in a system; e.g., vertically integrated systems or systems with shared facilities. In addition to the financial information, other relevant data such as the market conditions and competitive situation may not be available to the decision-makers.

A further barrier to disinvestment is the problem of management's goals conflicting with the overall economic goals of the company. Managers may not want to divest a subsidiary because of the stigma of failure which may be attached to the decision, personal identification with the subsidiary, concerns with community social welfare, or loss of prestige and/or compensation.

He further hypothesizes that these barriers to exit cause many firms to attempt to "turnaround" unprofitable subsidiaries instead of recognizing the need for disinvestment. The result of this is to squander management time as well as other resources.

With this foundation of domestic studies of disinvestment, it is now possible to turn to the studies of disinvestment of foreign subsidiaries to determine what additional factors in the international environment need to be considered.

Studies of Foreign Disinvestment

Two of the earliest articles on foreign disinvestment were by Hirschman and Behrman. Hirschman suggested that multinationals should have a planned program of disinvesting subsidiaries in developing countries.[11] Such disinvestment would foster the growth of the local developing economies. To accomplish this task, he proposed a series of methods including establishing an agency to act as an intermediary and arbitrator.

Behrman argued that such a program would result in a separation of host-country economies from the world economy.[12] He also argued that a program of planned disinvestment would reduce foreign investment and limit the transfer of technology. He reasoned that multinationals would not be willing to establish potential competitors.

These two articles concerned themselves only with the policy implications of multinational disinvestment. They did not examine the economics of specific subsidiaries.

Some of the earliest work done in the examination of specific disinvestments was done by Sachdev.[13] Concentrating on the subsidiaries of British multinational companies, he studied the magnitude and consequences of British disinvestment. Using data from the International Business Unit from the University of Manchester, he showed that although both gross British foreign investment and net investment were growing for the years through 1973, the difference between these two measures, the disinvestment gap, was widening.

He examined the role of disinvestment in several countries, notably India, Sri Lanka, and Pakistan, and noted the impact which disinvestment has had in these developing countries. Based on these studies of country disinvestment, he recommended several policy measures to reduce the adverse economic impacts of disinvestment.[14]

More importantly, for the purposes of this study, he also examined 21 case situations of disinvestment through interviews and questionnaires. He outlined several factors which influenced the decisions to disinvest.[15]

Of the financial factors, low profitability and losses were stated by managements as the main reason for disinvestment. Other financial factors cited were commercial difficulties, restrictions on funds transfers, and risks and uncertainties in the host country. A review of the other factors which were listed indicates that profitability of the subsidiary is a key element in the decision concerning disinvestment.[16]

Other factors were noted in addition, however. Organizational difficulties were cited in about one third of the cases, with communication channels problems cited as contributing to this problem. None of the companies involved had a formalized policy for dealing with the disinvestment situation, which resulted in ad hoc decisions being made. In almost all of the cases, the decision to disinvest was made by the chairman of the parent company, and in only one case was the foreign management of the subsidiary responsible for the decision.[17]

This study, although useful, is limited by the size of the survey sample and a bias in the companies selected. Only companies which had had at least one disinvestment characterized by adversity with the host government or with a trade union were included.

A study which overcomes these limitations was done by Torneden.[18] His study consisted of two major elements: a review of the magnitude of disinvestment by U.S. companies, and an examination of specific disinvestment cases.

His research, using the largest U.S. companies as listed on the Fortune 500, showed 561 foreign disinvestments between 1967-1971. This was approximately 16% of the number of new foreign subsidiaries established during that time period. This relationship showed an increasing trend, with disinvestment equaling 9.2% of new subsidiaries in 1967 and 36.7% in 1971. Of these disinvestments only 4% were expropriations. These statistics and others in his study parallel those indicated previously in this chapter based on the Harvard Multinational Enterprise Study.

His study of case situations of disinvestment included interviews with 15 companies and a questionnaire survey of another 38 companies. Based on this sample, he drew several conclusions:

1. A disinvestment decision was often preceded by a change in top management.
2. Top management was very involved in making the disinvestment decision as well as initially suggesting a disinvestment study. Subsidiary management rarely instigated the disinvestment review.
3. Most of the subsidiaries that were disinvested were not operating on an integrated or interconnected framework within the parent system.
4. The majority of the companies stated that the operations of the U.S. parent strongly influenced the decisions to invest or disinvest abroad.

Of those factors which were cited as reasons for disinvestment, an unacceptable return on investment was by far the most frequently mentioned. Other responses included too small a market and uncertain future for the product.

An additional work of note in the foreign disinvestment area was written by Boddewyn.[19] Although primarily a "how-to" monograph, stressing such aspects as negotiating positions and organizing for disinvestment, it does include some case studies of 40 disinvestment situations. These studies lack the detail of the Torneden work; however, in general the conclusions drawn from the studies are similar.

III. Scope of this Study

Building on these previous works, this study will provide additional information in an attempt to resolve the problems of why a particular subsidiary will be disinvested and when. Using the Harvard Multinational Enterprise Study data base will allow the analysis to encompass more subsidiaries than previous studies, thus overcoming one of their limitations.

The study will first examine the relevant theories of foreign direct investment in Chapter 2. Combining these theories and the work noted in the review of the previous studies will allow the development of a model of disinvestment in Chapter 3. Chapters 4 and 5 include the applications of this model to the subsidiaries included in the Harvard Multinational Enterprise Study data base. These chapters encompass the "testing" of the model.

Chapter 6 contains brief case studies of two disinvestments. The purpose of these cases is to examine the fit of the model in actual situations. The conclusions of the study are in Chapter 7.

2

Foreign Investment Theories

To develop a model of foreign disinvestment, it will first be useful to review the theories of foreign direct investment. Before a subsidiary can be disinvested, an initial investment must have occurred. In order to determine why the subsidiary might be divested, it will be helpful to have an understanding of the factors which influenced its creation.

Models and theories of foreign direct investment have been primarily based on manufacturing investment. Manufacturing investment was believed to more accurately reflect underlying economic factors than other types of investment; e.g., extractive activities which are dependent on the geographic location of raw materials. Thus these models, and this study as well, will focus on the manufacturing subsidiaries of multinational enterprises.

One of the earliest theories of direct foreign investment was developed by Hymer. He stated that foreign investment occurs for two reasons:

1. It is sometimes profitable to control enterprises in more than one country in order to remove competition between them.
2. Some firms have advantages in a particular activity, and they may find it profitable to exploit these advantages by establishing foreign operations.[1]

His investment model holds that foreign investment will occur only when there is some departure from the perfectly competitive market assumed in classical economic theory. Thus, he presupposed an oligopolistic industry structure as necessary for direct foreign investment.

He indicated that a local firm always has some advantages over a foreign firm operating in the host economy. These advantages include better information about the economy, laws, politics, etc., immunity from discrimination against foreign firms, and less concern with exchange rate fluctuations.

The foreign firm must possess some advantage over the local firm to enable it to complete. The foreign oligopolist may have superior marketing skills, access to lower cost factors of production, a more efficient production function, economies of scale, or a differentiated product. Any one or a combination of these advantages would allow the foreign competitor to compete in the local market. The imperfect market for these factors would restrict the local firm from purchasing them and improving its competitive abilities.[2]

Firms may compete with one another in local or third country markets. If such competition exists, it may be profitable to remove the element of competition and have a form of collusion.[3] One form of collusion is the creation of cartels; however, cartels are based on essentially voluntary agreements. Mergers provide better control and thus have become the most popular method. In these cases the larger firm, typically the U.S. company, emerges as dominant.

Following Hymer's theory, foreign direct investment can be classified into two categories: (1) active-investment to exploit a competitive advantage, and (2) reactive-investment to reduce competition.

I. Models of Active Foreign Direct Investment

A dynamic model of active foreign direct investment is the product life cycle theory proposed by Vernon.[4] This model holds that as a product is developed, it will encounter several distinct stages during its life cycle.

When a new product is first produced, it will normally be introduced in the home market of the innovating company. There are several reasons for this. First, since the product is new, there may be a need for product changes during its initial period of sales. Proximity to the market facilitates the required communication. Second, because it is an innovation, it will be relatively price inelastic, making low cost production less important than proximity to the market.

As the use of the product grows, foreign demand for the product will develop. This demand will be met by exports from the home country. This increased volume will allow for expanding economies of scale in production. Foreign firms will be prevented from producing the product because of barriers to entry, high costs for production and distribution in the small local markets, and lack of technology for the production process.

As the demand for the product increases abroad, the appeal of these foreign markets will increase. When the technology becomes available, foreign competitors may begin to produce the product for their home market. This threat of competition from other manufacturers will encourage the original producer to begin manufacturing in the foreign market.

The incentive to manufacture abroad will be additionally increased through tariffs. If tariff barriers prove to make exporting to a market less attractive because of the higher cost of the product in the market, the company may choose to manufacture inside the country, within the tariff walls, which would eliminate the tariff on the product. This elimination of the artificial tariff cost allows the firm to continue to compete in the local market and exploit its competitive advantages.

Moxon, in an effort to test investment theories empirically, examined offshore production in less-developed countries by U.S. electronics companies to manufacture items for shipment to the U.S.[5] He discovered that the initial investment in an offshore manufacturing facility was a response to competitive pressure. Primarily this was manifest in the form of price competition which usually resulted from imported products.

Stobaugh directed a group which studied the causes of nine foreign investments by U.S. multinational enterprises.[6] He concluded that the investments resulted from external pressures on the companies. These pressures were usually associated with holding or maintaining a position in an oligopolistic market. He also discovered that the primary competitors (other than U.S. firms) in these markets were not local firms, but rather non-U.S. multinationals.

A somewhat different model of active foreign direct investment was developed by Caves.[7] He proposed three possible reasons for overseas investments: the existence of intangible assets (such as trademarks) with no opportunity cost, the possibility of reducing the costs of production through the use of multiple plants, and the underutilization of entrepreneurial resources. In this model, a firm makes a voluntary choice to supplant its exports with foreign manufacturing in order to increase its return. Caves suggested that this action might not be forced by competitive actions, but rather reflect the firm's ability to exploit its advantages in the marketplace.

Another study of trade versus foreign direct investment was made by Horst.[8] He examined U.S. exports to Canada and the sales of U.S. subsidiaries in Canada. His initial results indicated that trade and subsidiary sales were supplementary. He also found, however, that the tariff structure significantly encouraged the establishment of subsidiaries. In conducting his study, one of his key assumptions was that Canadian firms did not have access to the technology of production which the subsidiaries of the U.S. companies possessed. His findings are thus consistent with the models of active foreign investment to exploit competitive advantages.

The competitive advantages which the multinational company may have are many. Horst's study indicates that the multinational firm may have access to technology which is not available to local competitors. Caves' model indicates that the multinational firm may have trademarks, economies of scale, and superior management abilities. Vernon's product life cycle model encompasses all of these factors and adds those which might accrue through initial product development, increased product knowledge and marketing abilities.

An additional competitive advantage of the multinational firms was hypothesized by Aliber.[9] He suggested that multinationals have an advantage over local firms in the capital markets. The market demands a premium for the exchange risk of foreign companies' earnings, but does not demand this exchange premium of the foreign earnings of the multinationals. The result is that multinationals have access to lower cost funds.

Another argument for the multinationals having access to lower cost funds is based on the portfolio theory of investments. This theory suggests that since the domestic economy may not be perfectly correlated with foreign economies, the inclusion of foreign investments in a portfolio may reduce the riskiness (variance) of the portfolio without reducing the expected return. This type of diversification of the risk may allow the multinational to operate with a lower cost of capital than local firms which are not similarly diversified.[10]

The models of active foreign direct investment hold that a multinational company has one or more of these competitive advantages. By investing in foreign manufacturing facilities the multinational can better exploit these advantages and increase its return.

However, as more competitors enter the market, the competitive advantage begins to be eroded. Other firms learn the technology of production; the market size expands to allow economies of scale to other firms; the marketing abilities of competitors increase, other firms gain access to the lower cost capital, etc.

As these competitors increase their ability to compete, the foreign company loses its advantage. The market share of the foreign company will decrease. Stobaugh, et al., noted this decline of market power for U.S. firms.[11] They found a gradual loss over time in the economic position of the U.S. within worldwide industries and subindustries.

The forces within the marketplace work to erode any competitive advantages and to equate all competing firms. At this stage in the life cycle, a product becomes a commodity, a non-differentiated product. The time frame in which this occurs depends upon the products. Some products arrive at the commodity status very rapidly, for example petrochemicals, while other companies attempt to prolong the life of their products through design changes, heavy advertising, and other methods. If a company is successful in these "holding actions" a product may never reach the commodity stage.

It is likely, however, that at some time, the product will no longer have any competitive advantages over other products in the market. Accompanying this loss of differentiation is the loss of the "excess rent" which the differentiation or competitive advantage allowed. With the decreased return for the subsidiary, the multinational no longer possesses the optimum portfolio of investments for its risk preference.

At this senescent stage, Vernon contends that the firm has two courses of action: drop the product or hang on.[12] If the firm chooses to hang on, it will be faced with price competition and low profit margins leading to a lower return and a less than optimal investment portfolio. Given this alternative, many companies have chosen to drop out after their competitive advantages were eroded. Examples of industries in which U.S. firms at one time had large foreign investments but since have withdrawn are electric power, life insurance, coffee plantations, and sugar plantations.[13]

Based on models of active foreign direct investment, the following can be hypothesized:

As the competition in a market increases, the probability of the disinvestment of a particular subsidiary operating in that market will also increase.

II. Models of Reactive Foreign Direct Investment

Reactive foreign direct investment means that a multinational company invests not necessarily to exploit a competitive advantage and thereby increase its return, but rather to prevent other firms from gaining a competitive advantage. This type of investment strategy could also be considered defensive in nature.

Building on the product life cycle theory, e.g. Knickerbocker hypothesized that firms exhibit a "follow-the-leader" strategy in making foreign investments.[14] Operating in an oligopolistic market structure, if the leader in an industry invests in a new market, the other members of the oligopoly will follow suit. By following the leader, the other firms minimize the risk that the leader will gain something from the new market which will upset the competitive balance.

A further model of foreign investment was developed by Graham.[15] His model describes what he terms "exchange of threat" behavior. A firm from Country A makes a foreign investment in Country B. This poses a threat to the home market of the local firm in Country B. Therefore, the company from Country B establishes a subsidiary in Country A. Thus an attempt is made to restore a competitive position and minimize the risk.

Both of these models suggest that reactive foreign investments are not based on an analysis of economic variables which might be reflected directly in the costs of the subsidiary. Instead, these investments are a result of the multinationals' perceptions of the activities and motivations of other competitors. In fact, the reactive investments might increase the direct costs of the multinational because of its investments in subsidiaries having no competitive advantages. However, the multinational is willing to incur these costs as a type of insurance policy against other competitive actions.

An associated role for the subsidiaries of multinationals following this risk minimization strategy is that of a listening post. The subsidiaries provide an important information network which allows the parent multinational to be informed of the activities of the other members of the oligopoly.

Since the process of investment in these reactive situations is based on risk minimization as opposed to profit maximization, the role of disinvestment in these models is difficult to predict. Certainly, the elimination of the risk would eliminate the need for the subsidiaries. However, in the oligopolistic markets of the multinationals, stability is very important and therefore the perceived need for subsidiaries may not wane.[16]

Another alternative would be for the multinational to disinvest subsidiaries when the cost of maintaining the subsidiary exceeded the perceived "return" of reduced risk. In other words, a company would decide that it could no longer afford to maintain the listening post or defensive position. In such a situation, the multinational would decide that the benefits provided by the subsidiary no longer warranted the costs of the subsidiary. This could occur through a reduction in perceived risk or because of higher return from alternative uses of the capital tied up in the subsidiary.

Both of these conditions result from factors within the multinational and are not necessarily direct reactions to external factors. The status of the subsidiaries is not totally independent of external factors, however. The increased return from alternative uses of the capital is at least partially related to the economic markets. The firm will compare this higher return with the risk of reduced stability through disinvesting.

Thus, the key variable is the firm's perception of risk. There are several external factors which could affect this. If another member of the oligopoly were to retrench in its foreign investments, the company could similarly disinvest in accordance with follow-the-leader behavior without risking a loss of stability. If new members begin to compete in the oligopoly, stability will be threatened by these actions and a company could disinvest without increasing the instability in the industry.

Based on these models of reactive foreign direct investment, the following can be hypothesized:

> As the risks of instability in a market are reduced, the probability of the disinvestment of a particular subsidiary operating in that market will increase.

III. Summary

Two modes of foreign direct investment have been proposed: active investment to capitalize on competitive advantages and reactive investment to reduce competition or maintain stability in the oligopoly. Each of these motivations for investment has different implications for the disinvestment process.

Since competitive advantages are the key aspects of active investment, disinvestment is not likely to occur until the multinational has lost these advantages. Typically, the advantages are eroded through actions in the market, and this is signalled by an increase in competition in the market. With the increased competition, profit margins will be reduced, and the subsidiary may be a candidate for disinvestment.

For reactive investments, the profit margins are not as important. These subsidiaries are established to reduce the multinational's perceived risk. Disinvestment is not likely until either the need for risk reduction is reduced or the return from the risk reduction is exceeded by returns from other investment alternatives.

Economic Evaluation of a Disinvestment

Following the patterns suggested by the theories of foreign direct investment, divestment analysis could be considered a type of investment decision in reverse. To determine the economic viability of a subsidiary, a firm should undertake a similar analysis to that done at the time of new capital investments. The relevant question for the parent is the value of continued operation of the subsidiary (cash flows) and the proceeds provided by disinvestment of the subsidiary.

I. Cash Flow Model of Disinvestment

A key factor in this type of analysis is the recognition that the subsidiary is only one element of the system. The impact on the cash flows throughout the system must be taken into consideration. This can be done by estimating the cash flows in the system with the existing subsidiary and those which would occur without the subsidiary. The difference in these cash flows is the relevant variable.

$$\text{Present Value of System Cash Flows} = \frac{CF}{(1 + k)} + \frac{CF_2}{(1 + k)^2} + \cdots \frac{CF_n}{(1 + k)^n}$$

In estimating the magnitude of the future cash flows, the company must consider the following factors:

1. The expected future operating cash flows. As noted above, the relevant cash flows may occur throughout the system and therefore be denominated in several currencies. These future flows will be influenced by several elements.
   a. The expected future profitability of the subsidiary. The future impact of current R&D and advertising expenditures must be estimated. The actions of competitors and their effect on profits needs to be forecast. This could include the possibility of new competitors as well. In addition, income from other sources such as royalties and management fees must be included.
      The impact of changes in technology must also be analyzed. If

a new technology is developed, will it make the subsidiary obsolete? Can the company improve the competitive position of the subsidiary by introducing new technology?

b. The impact of foreign exchange rate fluctuations. A change in the exchange rates may be reflected in the value of the cash flows of the subsidiary. The exchange rate is used not only in the translation of the cash flows into the parent currency, but it will also affect the costs of any imported materials used in production and perhaps even the price of the products. The company must therefore estimate future exchange rates to be included in the analysis.

c. The role of the host government. The political implications of operating in a foreign country are numerous. The host government can take actions which directly affect profitability, such as changing tax rates or mandating prices. Such changes could be taken by government in the country of the parent country as well. The additional multinational risks are actions to impose foreign exchange controls, limit repatriation of funds, limit foreign ownership, etc. Any of these actions could affect the future cash flows from the subsidiary.

2. The amount of non-cash expenses, particularly depreciation. The firm must determine whether the depreciation tax shield or allowance will continue to contribute to the cash flow in the future.

3. The need for additional investment. Any amounts required for investment to maintain equipment will need to be deducted from future cash flows; the alternative being to allow the machinery to run down. Any additional working capital requirements must also be included.

After isolating the relevant cash flows, the remaining element in the discounted cash flow analysis is the discount rate, the marginal cost of capital. Since the risk associated with this particular investment is the risk of the subsidiary which should be reflected in the cost of capital for the subsidiary, this cost is the appropriate measure to use.

The sum of the discounted cash flows, which is the present value of the cash flows to the parent, is then compared to the disinvestment value of the subsidiary. The disinvestment value is the amount which the company could receive if the subsidiary were sold or liquidated. If the disinvestment value exceeds the present value of the future cash flows to the parent, then disinvestment is economically justified.

Present Value of Cash Flows < Disinvestment Value

There are two factors which might cause a buyer to bid a price which is higher than the present value of the future cash flows for the seller. The discount rate for the buyer might be lower, or the projected cash flows might be higher.

The cash flows might be forecast at a higher level for several reasons. In addition to differences in future perceptions, the buying firm might also be able to benefit from increased economies of scale, both in technology and management, or from making use of underutilized resources. The buying firm might have management talent not fully utilized in current operations which could be used to develop a higher cash flow. The subsidiary could also complement other operations and provide a higher system cash flow for the buying company.

If the buyer is a local firm, other factors might be instrumental in causing the differences in the estimated future flows. The local firms in a market always possess some advantages over foreign competitors. These advantages could be familiarity with the market, knowledge of local language and customs, or perhaps favorable treatment from the government. At a minimum, the local company may not have to contend with translation gains and losses, repatriation limitations, or anti-foreign political actions.

As previously noted, in cases of active foreign investment the foreign subsidiaries possess some competitive advantage over the local companies and are able to earn some monopoly rent. As this competitive advantage is eroded, the monopoly rents will no longer be supported. With the local firms operating the subsidiaries, they might be able to achieve a higher cash flow because of their local advantages.

In disinvestments of subsidiaries established through active foreign investment, then, one would expect that the subsidiaries would be sold to local firms. This would be the case especially in countries where the governments were stressing local ownership through discriminatory taxes, limits on the repatriation of earnings, requirements for local ownership, etc. If the production inputs and the market for the output were located primarily in the local market, thereby eliminating the effect of foreign exchange rates on the local firm, the subsidiary would be additionally attractive to a local firm.

The study by Boddewyn of international disinvestments supports this hypothesis. In his review of 40 disinvestments, 27 of the subsidiaries were sold to local firms. Of the 10 which were sold to foreign firms, he reported that most of the firms were already operating in the country; they were not using the acquisition as a method of entry into the country.[1]

Even if cash flows might be projected at the same level for both the multinational and the local firm, a lower discount rate for the local company would yield a higher present value of the cash flows. The discount rate for the local firm might be lower for several reasons.

Since the local company might not have to contend with political risk, the total risk of the operations might be less. This would be reflected in a lower discount rate. If the local firm had access to lower cost sources of capital, for example through government guaranteed loans, the cost of capital or discount rate would be reduced.

In active foreign investment situations, where the subsidiary was established to exploit a competitive advantage, a buyer may be found through the external action of the marketplace. This will occur when the buyer projects higher cash flows from the subsidiary or has a lower discount rate. These conditions are made possible through the changing competitive environment.

For those subsidiaries which are established as reactive foreign investments, the scenario may be somewhat different. Certainly, changes in the competitive environment could allow the situation described above to occur. It is more likely, however, that the changes will occur within the parent company.

Where the investment is made to protect the cash flows of other subsidiaries in the system, the relevant cash flows in the disinvestment decision will greatly exceed those associated directly with the subsidiary. With the large cash flows, the present value to the parent would exceed the value to a buyer which did not have the associated cash flow concerns.

If the parent perceives a change in the environment, for instance, that the oligopoly's stability is no longer directly related to maintaining the subsidiary, then the relevant cash flows become smaller. The cash flows elsewhere in the system would not be as exposed if the subsidiary were disinvested. Thus the reduced magnitude of cash flows included in the analysis would result in a lower present value of the cash flows. As these relevant cash flows are reduced, the potential for finding an acceptable selling price is increased.

Another alternative for the evaluation of the disinvestment is a change in the discount rate. As noted in the discussion of reactive foreign direct investments, a multinational will continue to operate a subsidiary in the hope of maintaining stability in the oligopoly as long as it can afford to do so. This implies that the subsidiary will be operated as long as the multinational cannot invest its funds in projects with higher returns. As the opportunity cost of funds increases, the discount rate applied to the subsidiaries' cash flows will increase as well. With an increased discount rate, the present value of the cash flows will be less. The higher discount rate might allow a buyer with a lower discount rate to offer a purchase price for the subsidiary which exceeds the present value of the cash flows to the parent. This could occur even though the buyer would not be including the system cash flows which the parent would include.

In the case of subsidiaries established through reactive foreign direct investment, the present value model is also applicable. The adjustments in the environment needed to facilitate disinvestment may, however, result from the multinational's internal perceptions as well as from external factors in the marketplace.

II. Issues in Application of the Cash Flow Model

In applying the present value model of disinvestment, one of the prime considerations is the evaluation of the relevant cash flow. As previously noted, the cash flows which directly result from the operations of a subsidiary are not the only cash flows to include in the analysis. Those cash flows in other associated subsidiaries must also be taken into account.

For those subsidiaries which were established to exploit a competitive advantage, the determination of the relevant cash flows is easier. In this case, the subsidiary may indeed be isolated from the other elements of the system. Even if not, the impact on the demand and/or supply prices of the associated subsidiaries may be a straightforward calculation.

A complicating factor in this situation is the subsidiary's sharing of production factors with other subsidiaries, especially marketing and distribution facilities. The disinvestment of a subsidiary might not reduce the overhead or fixed costs which the parent has invested throughout the system. Thus the products sold by other subsidiaries would have to bear a higher price to compensate for the lower system volume. The impact of these higher prices on the cash flows in the other elements of the system would need to be included.

For those subsidiaries which were established as a reactive measure to maintain stability in the oligopoly, the relevant cash flows are obviously more difficult to determine. In this case, not only those subsidiaries which are associated through shared facilities, but perhaps all of the subsidiaries' cash flows are affected. Thus, the determination of the magnitudes of the cash flows may rest on the perceptions of management.

It is also obvious that for a parent to disinvest a subsidiary, there must be some disinvestment value. For the transaction to take place, there must be a buyer for the subsidiary, either as a going enterprise or on a liquidation of assets basis. This means that the assets of the subsidiary must be transferable to the buyer.

If the assets are specific to the subsidiary or parent corporation, they will have reduced value to an outsider. This is true whether the specific assets are tangible—specialized equipment or inventories—or intangible—brand names and trademarks. The more specific assets a subsidiary possesses, the more likely it is that present value of the cash flows from those assets to the parent will exceed the value of the assets to a potential buyer.

One would expect, therefore, that subsidiaries possessing specific assets would be less likely to be disinvested, all other factors being equal. Since these assets have greater value to the parent than to another company, it is less likely that another company will bid a sufficiently high price for them to exceed the present value of the cash flows which they could generate for the parent.

Both of these problems of application of the cash flow model are based on economic considerations. Another issue, management, is not an economic concern but rather a problem of management reaching a decision and carrying out the disinvestment. Disinvestment decisions seem to be difficult decisions for management and are often made long after the economics of a situation justified the disinvestment.

There seem to be several reasons why managers have difficulty in making disinvestment decisions:

1. Maximizing the net present value of cash flows may not be the corporate objective. The calculation of the discounted cash flows assumes that the managers are attempting to maximize the stock price of the firm through increasing the present value of the assets (subsidiaries) which it holds. Indeed, there may be other factors which the management is attempting to maximize.

   Since the actual price of a subsidiary is related to its economic value (discounted cash flows), it may not have any relationship to the value of the subsidiary which the parent system is carrying on its financial statements. Any difference between the selling price and the book value will be shown on the ensuing financial statements as a book loss on the disinvestment. Management may believe that showing a book loss will allow criticism of their management ability or perhaps indicate to investors a lack of managerial ability.

   The firm may be following a goal of maximizing the growth of earnings per share or the size of the company. The disinvestment of a subsidiary might well cause a drop in the earnings for the entire system. Even though this might only be a temporary decline, management might believe that this decrease could have an adverse impact on the public's perception of the company.

2. Managers may be maximizing their own goals rather than those of the firm. They may be attempting to minimize individual risk in their own careers. Thus they would be hesitant to recommend or take any actions which might increase the personal risk which they face in their own career development.

   There may be no incentive for the subsidiary manager to recommend disinvestment. Typical management control systems and incentive systems do not reward disinvestment recommendations. Given this, the manager would be adding an element of uncertainty into his professional life with no expected increased return. A recommendation of disinvestment might be viewed by top management as a chance to rid themselves of the manager. A native manager of a subsidiary might feel especially vulnerable in this situation.

Disinvestment may be viewed as an admission of failure by the manager. The prevailing view among managers is that a "good" manager can turn around a bad situation. Thus a recommendation of disinvestment is viewed as an admission by the manager that he has failed.

Often, disinvestments cause social problems in the local economy. The disinvestment of a subsidiary might cause unemployment and economic hardship in a country or community. A manager, particularly a native, might not want to inflict these problems on his community.

Even top level management is not immune to this individual risk minimizing behavior. Although the top managers are not involved in the daily operations of the subsidiary, they nevertheless feel responsible for it. Disinvestment may again be viewed as evidence that they are unable to effectively manage the company.

3. Another barrier to disinvestment is the identification which managers develop with subsidiaries. As this identification becomes stronger, managers are more hesitant to disinvest the subsidiary. Factors which seem to heighten this sense of identification are the length of time the subsidiary has been part of the system, the relative size of the subsidiary, newly formed subsidiaries as opposed to acquisitions, and location in economies similar to the home country's.

All of these management factors can be summarized as conflicting goals.[2] The goals of the managers differ from the economic best interests of the company.

Another problem is that typically companies do not have staff personnel assigned to disinvestment analysis as they do for capital budgeting and other investment decisions. As a result the decisions are made on an ad hoc basis with little commonality of analysis or informational input. Gilmour, in his study of domestic disinvestments, noted that any data analysis which was done in those decisions was done after the decision to disinvest had already been made and was undertaken to justify the decision.[3]

It can be postulated that the more often a company faces a disinvestment decision, the better prepared the company will be to handle it. Thus, companies who have made few disinvestments find that lack of experience in gathering and processing the necessary data is a barrier.

Lest the impact of these managerial barriers be lessened, it is important to note that both Gilmour's study[4] and Torneden's study[5] indicated that changes of top management were needed before economically justifiable disinvestments were undertaken. The new managements had no commitment to the subsidiaries, nor did they feel responsible for their lack of profitability.

Because of the size of the multinationals, unprofitable subsidiaries can easily be "hidden" so long as other subsidiaries and the parent company are sufficiently profitable. Torneden noted, in the case studies which he undertook, that in all of the cases the subsidiaries were not disinvested until the profits of the U.S. parent began to fall.[6] With growing earnings, there is no pressure to disinvest poorly performing subsidiaries. However, once the overall performance of the company slackens, then the company will feel constrained to disinvest the unprofitable elements.

This constraint will occur for two reasons. First, the poorly performing subsidiary will have a detrimental impact on the system earnings, and disinvestment will remove this earnings drain. Second, disinvestment will provide cash for the parent to use in supporting its other operations. This cash might not be available in the capital markets because of the falling performance of the parent system.

III. The Disinvestment Model

The discounted cash flow approach to disinvestment decisions suggests that disinvestment should occur when the disinvestment value of the subsidiary exceeds the present value of the cash flows generated through continued operation.

$$\text{Disinvestment Value} > \sum_{n=1} \frac{CF_n}{(1 + k)^n}$$

As discussed previously, there are two factors which could increase the likelihood of the disinvestment value exceeding the cash flows: a reduction in the cash flows or an increase in the discount rate. On the other hand, there are several factors which would lessen the likelihood of a subsidiary's disinvestment: interdependence of subsidiaries, possession of specific assets, and conflicting management goals. Thus, for any specific subsidiary, the likelihood or probability of disinvestment is a function of those factors which encourage disinvestment and those which discourage it. This function can be formulated as follows:

$$p(D) = f(CF, k, I, SA, CMG)$$

Where:

$p(D)$ = Probability of disinvestment of the subsidiary
CF = Expected future cash flows associated with the subsidiary
k = Discount rate for the subsidiary

I   = Interdependence of subsidiary with system
SA   = Level of specific assets in the subsidiary
CMG = Existence of conflicting goals within the management system

A reduction in the expected cash flows associated with a subsidiary will increase the probability of the subsidiary's disinvestment. Such a reduction increases the likelihood of the present value of the cash flows equaling or being less than the disinvestment value. This does not imply that any reduction in cash flows will result in the subsidiary's being disinvested, but rather that the possibility of disinvestment is increased.

In addition to the cash flows, the discount rate for the subsidiary is also instrumental in determining the present value of the subsidiary. An increase in the discount rate will result in a lower present value which in turn increases the probability of disinvestment.

For subsidiaries established to exploit competitive advantages, it is likely that the cash flows will be reduced as competition in the market is increased. For reactive investments, the discount rate may be adjusted upward as the opportunity rate in the company increases or the relevant cash flows may be reduced as the company perceives that other activities in the system are not as exposed to industry instability. Either or both of these factors could lead to a change in the likelihood of disinvestment.

In applying the cash flow analysis to a subsidiary, it is possible that the isolation of the cash flows associated with that subsidiary will be difficult. This may be caused by the interdependence of the subsidiary with other activities within the parent system. The greater this interdependence, the less likely it is that the model will be applied. If it is applied, then because of the interdependence, the cash flows and resultant present value of the subsidiary are likely to be higher to the parent than to a potential purchaser.

A similar problem of valuation is caused by the specific assets which a subsidiary possesses. Since these assets are specific to the subsidiary or parent system, they are likely to have greater value to the subsidiary than to a buyer or if sold through liquidation. The specific assets do not affect the cash flow analysis as such, but rather indicate that the probable disinvestment value for the subsidiary will be lower than in their absence.

The remaining factor in the model is conflicting management goals. If the goals of management are such that the discounted cash flow analysis is not used, of course the model is of little use in describing the probability of disinvestment. It is more likely, however, that although using the model, management may choose not to accept its results. Managers may attempt to "turn around" a poorly performing subsidiary rather than accept a stigma of failure. In these situations of conflicting goals, disinvestment is less likely to occur.

The hypothesized impact of each of the factors in the model is shown in Table 3-1.

This model follows the previous work of Caves and Porter in examining the disinvestment decisions of specific subsidiaries. However, the model places the decision in the context of the strategy of the parent and the life cycle of the subsidiary.

Evaluation of the cash flows and discount rate involves the consideration of the initial investment strategy. For active investments, the comparative advantages and competitive positions are essential elements in the analysis. For those subsidiaries established for reactive purposes, the firm's perceptions of risk and industry stability must be considered.

The other three factors in the model basically follow the hypotheses of the Caves and Porter work.

IV. Summary

The disinvestment decision should be based on a discounted cash flow analysis. The value of the discounted future cash flows from operating the subsidiary should be compared to the proceeds from disinvesting. If the disinvestment proceeds exceed the value of the future cash flows, the subsidiary should be disinvested.

This framework of analysis holds for both types of subsidiaries, active and reactive investments. The differences between these two are that the changes in conditions for disinvestment of subsidiaries formed through active investment come about primarily through economic forces in the market. Reactive investments may also require changes in the multinational's perceptions of risk and oligopolistic stability.

In application, the cash flow method encounters several difficulties. Isolating the relevant cash flows, while conceptually simple, is pragmatically difficult. In addition, the problem of assets which are specific to the subsidiary and not readily transferable may lessen the potential disinvestment value of the subsidiary.

Besides these two economic issues, a major problem confronting the cash flow model is the willingness of management to make disinvestment decisions. Managers may be using other decision criteria, such as maximizing growth, rather than maximizing the net present value of cash flows. Alternatively, managers may be pursuing their own goals rather than the objectives of the firm.

Because of these problems, managers may avoid making disinvestment decisions. In these cases, additional factors, such as a drop in overall system earnings or a change in management, may be needed to facilitate the disinvestment process.

Table 3-1

Hypothesized Impact of Disinvestment Model

Model: p (D) = f(CF, k, I, SA, CMG)
Where:

p(D)	=	Probability of disinvestment of subsidiary
CF	=	Expected future cash flows
k	=	Discount rate
I	=	Interdependence of subsidiary
SA	=	Level of specific assets
CMG	=	Conflicting management goals

Change in Factor	Hypothesized Change in p (D)
Reduction in CF	Increase
Increase in k	Increase
Higher level of I	Reduction
Higher level of SA	Reduction
Higher level of CMG	Reduction

Combining all of these factors, a disinvestment model was hypothesized.

$$p\,(D) \;=\; f\,(CF, k, I, SA, CMG)$$

This model suggests that the probability of disinvestment for a subsidiary is a function of cash flows, discount rate, interdependence, specific assets, and conflicting management goals.

4

Tests of the Disinvestment Model

Having developed and explained the model of foreign subsidiary disinvestment, the next step is to examine the patterns of disinvestment to determine whether they fit the prescriptions of the model. Using the probability function developed in Chapter 3, the characteristics of subsidiaries will be examined to determine whether the subsidiaries which were disinvested have those characteristics described by the model.

$$p(D) = f(CF, k, I, SA, CMG)$$

I. The Data Base

A substantial amount of data on the subsidiaries of U.S. based multinational companies has been accumulated by the Harvard Multinational Enterprise Study. This study has isolated 187 U.S. based companies which appeared in the *Fortune* 500 in 1963 or 1964 and had manufacturing subsidiaries in 6 or more foreign countries in 1965 or before.[1]

Originally this study covered the years through 1967; however, the data was recently updated through 1975. Since this addition provided more complete data and covers the most recent period, it was used to trace the patterns of disinvestment for the purpose of testing the disinvestment model.

However, several adjustments were made to the data to provide a more useful analysis.

1. Since the primary thrust of this study is to examine the "voluntary" disinvestment of subsidiaries, those subsidiaries which left the parent system because of expropriation or nationalization were not included.

   In these cases the company does not have any choice in the matter and probably does not undertake an analysis of the disinvestment. For this reason, expropriations have been eliminated from the sample for analysis.

   Forced sales, although similar in nature, unfortunately are not identified on the data bases and are included in the sample. A recent study by Robinson found that although there is a growing movement to force divestiture of equity in some manufacturing functions, it has not led to large scale disinvestments.[2] This is apparently due to the continued dependence of many countries on foreign capital and technology. Thus, this problem may become increasingly important in the future; however, its impact so far may not have been significant.

2. Only subsidiaries which were engaged in manufacturing activities were included. The model is based on the concept of manufacturing products in foreign subsidiaries as explained in Chapter 2. If extractive, sales, or service subsidiaries were included, the pattern of disinvestment might be distorted. One would not expect that the motivations for nor the analysis of disinvestment of a mining operation would be the same as for a manufacturing facility, due to the geographic orientation. Additionally, many sales and service subsidiaries may be only "shell" subsidiaries established as tax shelters or for similar purposes. These subsidiaries by their nature are transitory and would be disinvested for completely different reasons than a manufacturing subsidiary.

3. Subsidiaries which are not majority owned, 51% or greater, by the U.S. parent were not included. This is done because the inherent instability of minority owned or 50-50 joint ventures would affect the disinvestment pattern. Various studies have shown that this type of ownership structure is very unstable.[3] In these subsidiaries disinvestment may occur because of discontent with the joint partner and not because of the economic situation.

Based on these adjustments, the data base consisted of the subsidiaries which manufactured products during the 1968-1975 period, were majority owned by the U.S. parent, and were sold or liquidated if disinvested. Disinvestment will be defined to have occurred if the subsidiary is totally eliminated from the system. This eliminates the partial disinvestments caused by governmental mandates in countries such as India and Mexico. Active subsidiaries are those which were not disinvested and continued in operation as of December 31, 1975.

One aspect of disinvestment cannot be directly determined from the data base. A company may change the product manufactured by the subsidiary rather than disinvesting the subsidiary. Such an action could be called product disinvestment as opposed to subsidiary disinvestment. Such a change is difficult to ascertain from the data compiled on the subsidiaries. Because of the lack of data on product disinvestment, there is no way to predict its impact on the analysis. Although an attempt was made to address this issue in the analysis it undoubtedly contributed to the residuals or unexplained variance in the statistical analysis.

Not all disinvestments are expected to follow the suggested long-term disinvestment pattern. Some disinvestments may occur as error corrections. For example, a company makes a strategic error in establishing a subsidiary or in acquiring another company.[4] As this error becomes evident through poor performance, the company will move to rectify the situation. The actions that could be taken include disinvestment.

Despite the fact that this disinvestment would not occur as a result of long-term economic developments, the firm should still undertake the same type of discounted cash flow analysis. Thus, even though the cause for the disinvestment in this situation differs from the pattern suggested by the life cycle pattern, the economic analysis and the problems of exit barriers and resistance to disinvestment might be the same.

With these caveats, the adjustments to the data base resulted in 5,037 subsidiaries which met the criteria. Of these, 481 were disinvested during the 1968-1975 time period and 4,556 continued active operations at the end of 1975. The data on these subsidiaries formed the data base used to examine the patterns of disinvestment.

One of the problems of the data base is that it includes only cross-sectional data. For each subsidiary, there is only one observation for each of several variables. The data base does not include any information about changes over time for the subsidiaries.

The proposed disinvestment model is essentially a longitudinal model. It hypothesizes that over time, changes will occur which will reduce the value of the subsidiary to the parent, increase the value to a potential buyer, or a combination of both. It was hypothesized that as certain variables change, the likelihood of disinvestment would increase.

The cross-sectional data does not allow for direct tests of these hypotheses. Using this data only allows conclusions about the impact on disinvestment of subsidiaries of levels or values of the variables. It does not allow tests of whether the variables change in value over time.

Other studies have, however, demonstrated that the hypothesized relationships change over time, especially the cash flows and discount rates which are affected by the competitive environment in a market. Knickerbocker found that the competition in foreign markets tended to increase over time.[5] His study demonstrated a marked increase in the number of multinational companies, both U.S. and foreign, competing in foreign product markets. In addition to these multinational competitors, there are likely to be local producers in the markets, although his study did not address this issue.

Using his study as a basis for support for the concept of changing conditions over time, the use of cross-sectional data in the tests is warranted. Since he demonstrated that the factors undergo changes, the cross-sectional tests can be used to determine if the propensity to disinvest is affected by the different values of the variables. In other words, his study showed that a variable might move from value A to value B. A cross-sectional analysis would indicate whether at value B a subsidiary was more likely to be disinvested than at value A.

II. The Variables

Disinvestment as Related to Cash Flow and Discount Rate

The disinvestment model hypothesized that as the cash flows from a subsidiary were reduced, or if the discount rate were increased, the probability of disinvestment of that subsidiary would increase. Ideally, to test this hypothesis, an examination of the cash flows and discount rates of the subsidiaries would be undertaken. Unfortunately, data on the internal cash flows and discount rates for the subsidiaries is not available. As a result, proxies for these factors needed to be used.

The economic evaluation of disinvestments in Chapters 2 and 3 suggested that an increasing number of competitors in a market signaled a reduction of the foreign subsidiaries competitive advantages and thereby a lowering of the cash flows that the subsidiary produced. In addition, for those subsidiaries established for reactive purposes, an increase in the competitors would indicate increased instability in a market and would reduce the need for the maintenance of a subsidiary to provide a defensive position. Thus, the level of competition in a market may be used as a proxy for reduced cash flows and/or increased discount rate.

A high level of competition is hypothesized to increase the likelihood of a subsidiary's disinvestment. This means that given two subsidiaries, all other factors being equal, the subsidiary in the industry with the higher level of competition would be more likely to be disinvested.

Data on the competitors in foreign markets is also not readily available. Using the Harvard Multinational Enterprise Study data, one could determine the number of U.S. based competitors operating in a given market. However, there may be also non-U.S. based multinational companies and local firms competing in the market.

The Harvard Multinational Enterprise Study has compiled data on non-U.S. based multinational companies, but only through 1971.[6] In addition, non-multinational local companies are not included in any of these data bases, nor is information on them readily available from other sources. Thus, useful information on the number of competitors in foreign markets is not accessible.

As a means of approximating the number of competitors in foreign markets, the level of competition in U.S. markets was used as a proxy. The level of competition was assumed to be represented by the percentage of total value of shipments in an industry accounted for by the eight largest firms in that industry.[7] This assumes that those industries with a high percentage of shipments accounted for by the largest eight firms have less competition or fewer competitors. The industries were segmented at the four digit Standard Industrial Classification Code level. For convenience, this variable will subsequently be referred to as the industry concentration level.

The use of the U.S. industry concentration data also assumes that the level of competition within industries in foreign markets approximates that in the U.S. Various studies have indicated a similarity betwen U.S. concentration levels and those of other industrialized countries, namely the United Kingdom, West Germany, France, and Japan.[8] It is unlikely, however, that the concentration levels for non-industrialized countries, particularly LDC's, would be similar to those in the U.S. This problem was considered in the analysis which follows.

In analyzing the industry concentrations, it is important to note that a high level of shipments value accounted for by the eight largest firms in the industry is assumed to mean that there are fewer competitors in the market. As a result, the probability of disinvestment of a subsidiary is postulated to vary inversely to the total value of shipments represented by the eight largest firms in the industry. Thus, a high value for the variable would be assumed to mean low competition and a low probability of disinvestment.

Since the use of the level of competition in the U.S. is a third level of approximation for the cash flows and discount rates for the subsidiaries, another method was used to isolate economically justified disinvestments. It was assumed that if a disinvestment occurred in an industry, it was an indication that disinvestment was feasible for all subsidiaries in that industry. Therefore, if no disinvestments occurred in an industry, it was assumed that the cash flows and discount rates in that industry did not warrant disinvestment and all subsidiaries in that industry were excluded from the data base.

This further adjustment to approximate economically justified disinvestments resulted in a total of 3,795 subsidiaries in the data base of which 474 were disinvested.

As previously noted, one of the complicating factors in this analysis is product disinvestment—the disinvestment of a product rather than the subsidiary. With a single product subsidiary, if the product performs poorly, the subsidiary will perform poorly. If the subsidiary has several products, the cash flows are not as dependent on a single product. From an economic standpoint, it would be more likely that the product would be disinvested rather than the subsidiary. It is, therefore, expected that subsidiaries with more than one product would be less likely to be disinvested. Thus, another variable used as proxy for economic justification of a disinvestment was the number of products, as defined by different SIC codes, produced by a subsidiary.

Disinvestment as Related to Interdependence

The model hypothesizes that interdependence of the subsidiary with other activities within the parent system will mitigate against disinvestment of the subsidiary. This results from difficulties in isolating the relevant cash flows or from the impact on cash flows in other subsidiaries. This latter effect would lead to a higher present value to the parent system than to a potential purchaser or from liquidation.

One aspect of interdependence, the strategic element of reactive investment, has been discussed previously. The interdependence which is being considered with this factor is the operational interdependence of shared facilities, distribution channels, etc. The strategic relationships are considered part of the cash flow and discount rate factors.

In order to accurately determine the operational interaction between subsidiaries, internal information on the activities within a system is required. This information is not available for this study. Therefore, a proxy must be used.

One method of estimating the interdependence of the subsidiary is to examine the amount of sales made by the subsidiary within the system. It can be postulated that subsidiaries with a higher level of sales to other elements of the system will be more interrelated. This may result from the subsidiary producing intermediate products which are used as inputs elsewhere in the system. The disinvestment of such subsidiaries would create supply problems elsewhere in the system. Thus, one would expect a greater likelihood of disinvestment of those subsidiaries with primarily an external market.

Disinvestment as Related to Specific Assets

The disinvestment model postulates that the presence of specific assets in the subsidiary will reduce the likelihood of the subsidiary's disinvestment. These assets will lower the value of the subsidiary to other potential owners, thereby reducing the price they would be willing to pay for the subsidiary. What is actually happening is not a problem of application of the discounted cash flow model but rather a reduction of the potential purchase price.

As an example, two subsidiaries with identical book values of the assets are assumed. However, one subsidiary possesses assets which are of a more specific nature and relate to other products within the parent system, such as dies for unique parts. All other things being equal, the subsidiary with the specific assets would probably have less value to other owners, and therefore the potential purchase price would be lower. If the forecasted cash flows for the two subsidiaries were equal, the subsidiary with the more specific assets would be less likely to be divested.

One possible method of examining the impact of the specific and durable assets is to compare the assets of a subsidiary with its sales. If a subsidiary has a high assets/sales ratio, it means that the product is more asset or capital intensive. This would increase the possibility of having specific assets. Those subsidiaries with a low assets/sales ratio would be less capital intensive, and the the likelihood of specific assets would be less.

Disinvestment as Related to Conflicting Management Goals

One of the reasons for lack of disinvestment when it is economically justified is that managements have difficulty in making the decision to disinvest. This inability or difficulty in decision-making can result from any of several circumstances: failure to maximize the net present value of the firms' assets, minimizing individual career risk, or personal identification with subsidiaries.

To properly evaluate the role that these factors play in the disinvestment decision, one should analyze the decision-making process on an individual basis. This would, of course, require detailed information on the individuals who were involved in a disinvestment or nondisinvestment decision. Such a review, while perhaps possible, is beyond the scope of this study which is based on external data collected on the subsidiaries.

It is possible, however, to examine which subsidiaries were disinvested, and relate the pattern of disinvestment to proxies for these management barriers. This would be particularly appropriate in analyzing the aspect of management identification with subsidiaries. One would expect that those subsidiaries which had attributes allowing the greatest amount of individual identification would show the lowest rates of disinvestment. Subsidiaries which would provide less management identification would have higher disinvestment.

The identification of management with particular subsidiaries could come through a number of channels. Top management might have been involved with a subsidiary in early years. The subsidiary might have been nursed through difficult times or situations at a considerable cost of management time and effort. Managers might be more concerned about large subsidiaries because of the magnitude of their contribution to the system. Managers might identify with subsidiaries located in particular countries, perhaps because of the manager's ancestry or a particular interest. Three aspects of this identification lend themselves to external measurement: the size of the subsidiary, its method of entry into the system, and the length of time in the system.

Subsidiaries which are newly formed will often require more management time than those which are acquired. Because of the effort expended on starting these subsidiaries, the psychological attachment of management to those subsidiaries will be greater. Because of this greater attachment, those subsidiaries which were newly formed would be expected to have a lower probability of disinvestment.

Subsidiaries with larger sales amounts would provide greater potential for identification because of the significance of their operations to the total of the system. The subsidiary might not be interrelated with other affiliates but its size alone might be a barrier to disinvestment. Small subsidiaries could be disinvested with less difficulty because of fewer personnel being affected, small amounts of funds involved, and less impact on the system's financial statements. Large disinvestments might greatly affect the reported sales of the system. For managers who might be compensated in relation to sales or who prefer managing larger organizations, the reduction in sales might be a deterrent to disinvestment. Thus, it is expected that large subsidiaries are less likely to be disinvested than small ones.

The longer that a subsidiary has been in the system, the greater the opportunity for management to develop an identification with the subsidiary. Recent additions to the system will not have developed the sense of identification and would be easier to disinvest. A long time in the system is, therefore, expected to be a deterrent to disinvestment.

III. Test Results

To analyze the effects of these variables on the probability of disinvestment, a series of logistic regressions were run. The logistic regression model fits an S-shaped, or logistic, curve to the data.[9] Since the dependent variable has a value of either 1, when the subsidiary was disinvested, or 0, when disinvestment did not occur, the dependent variable of the model expresses the probability that disinvestment will or will not occur.

The general formulation of the model is as follows:

$$\log_e \frac{p}{1-p} = \beta_0 + \beta_1 X_1 + \beta_2 X_2 + \beta_n X_n$$

where p = "true" but uncertain long run fraction of subsidiaries which will be disinvested.

Using this model, each of the variables was examined individually, and then a multiple regression was used to examine the collective impact on the probability of disinvestment.

For each of the regression runs, any subsidiaries with missing data for the relevant variables were excluded. The number of subsidiaries included in the data base (n) is shown for each regression equation as is the number of subsidiaries which were disinvested.

Percent of Total Value of Shipments Accounted for by Eight Largest Firms in the Industry—Industry Concentration

This variable was used as a proxy for estimating when disinvestments were justified by cash flow or discount rate considerations. It was hypothesized that a higher industry concentration would indicate lower competition in that industry and a lower probability of disinvestment of subsidiaries in the industry.

The regression results were as follows:

$$p(D) = -1.80 \quad -.003\,(X1)$$
$$(1.0)^{10} \quad (.89)$$
$$R^2 = .01$$
$$n = 3795$$

No. of disinvestments = 474

where $X1$ = the concentration ratio for the subsidiary's industry with a range from 5 to 100.

As expected, subsidiaries in industries with low levels of competition, as represented by high percentages of industry concentration, exhibited less likelihood of disinvestment.

The results also show, however, that there is an 11% chance that the sign of the coefficient could be positive. This coupled with the low R^2 does not allow a high degree of confidence in the results.

It is important to note that the use of this variable assumed industry structures similar to the U.S. in other markets. The obvious problems of this assumption could partially explain the low R^2 for the regression.

Number of Different Products Produced by the Subsidiary

This variable was also used as a proxy for when disinvestment was justified. Since product disinvestment is an alternative to subsidiary disinvestment, those subsidiaries manufacturing several products were expected to have a lower probability of disinvestment. This was supported by the regression results.

$$p(D) = -1.40 \quad -.33\,(X2)$$
$$(1.0) \quad (1.0)$$
$$R^2 = .02$$
$$n = 3795$$

No. of disinvestments = 474

where $X2$ = the number of different SIC codes in which the subsidiary manufactured products which ranged from 1 to 6.

The expected relationship was shown. The regression equation indicates that those subsidiaries which have more products have a lower probability of disinvestment. The high probability of sign of the estimate of the variable, 1.0, indicates that the distribution of the estimates of the coefficient was entirely negative. Thus, even though the R^2 is low, the postulated relationship is very strongly supported.

Level of Intrasystem Sales

This variable was used as a proxy for interdependence of the subsidiary with other activities within the parent system. The disinvestment model postulated that disinvestment of those subsidiaries which were more interdependent would be less likely. The results of the regression support this hypothesis.

$$p\,(D) = \begin{array}{cc} -1.30 & -1.4\,(X3) \\ (1.0) & (1.0) \end{array}$$

R^2 = .08
n = 3665
No. of disinvestments = 444
where X3 = the level of sales by the subsidiary which was segmented
                    into three groups in the data base based on the following:
1 — less than 10% of sales to other activities within the system
2 — 10%-50% of sales within the system
3 — over 50% of sales within the system

As hypothesized, a higher level of intrasystem sales resulted in a lower probability of disinvestment. The high probability of the sign indicates a high degree of confidence in the statistical relationship. Although the R^2 is not very high, it is better than the other variables, and coupled with the high probabilty of sign allows a high degree of confidence in the results.

Assets/Sales Ratio

The disinvestment model hypothesized that subsidiaries possessing specific assets would be less likely to be disinvested. The assets/sales ratio was used as a surrogate for the specific assets in a subsidiary. It was postulated that subsidiaries with a high assets/sales ratio, i.e. those that were more capital intensive, would be likely to have more specific assets and thus have a lower likelihood of disinvestment. This relationship was shown by the regression results.

$$p\,(D) = \begin{array}{cc} -2.8 & -.05\,(X4) \\ (1.0) & (.55) \end{array}$$

R^2 = .01

n   = 2600

No. of disinvestments = 140

where X4 = a ratio of the level of assets and sales. The actual assets and sales amounts were not included in the data base, rather the following levels for each were given.

1. Less than US $1 million
2. US $1-US $10 million
3. US $10-US $25 million
4. US $25-US $100 million
5. Over US $100 million

The value of X4 therefore ranged from 1/5 to 5/1.

Although the regression equation shows the expected relationship— higher assets/sales ratio indicating a lower probability of disinvestment—the low probability of sign of the coefficient and the low R^2 suggest very weak support for the hypothesis.

Method of Entry of the Subsidiary

The disinvestment model suggested that conflicting management goals would mitigate against disinvestment of subsidiaries. Subsidiaries which entered the system by being newly formed were postulated to have more opportunities for conflicting management goals; therefore, disinvestment of such subsidiaries would be less likely.

$$p\,(D) = \quad -2.99 \qquad +.26\,(X5)$$
$$\qquad\qquad (1.0) \qquad\quad (.93)$$
$$R^2 \quad = .01$$
$$n \quad = 3665$$

No. of disinvestments = 444

where X5 = a dummy variable with a value of 0 for subsidiaries which were newly formed and a value of 1 for those subsidiaries which were acquired.

As hypothesized, there was a higher probability of disinvestment for those subsidiaries which had been acquired. Although the R^2 indicates that very little of the variance of the data was explained, the .93 probability of sign is relatively high. Thus, the hypothesis received moderate support from the results.

Subsidiary Sales

Another suggested method for examining the possibility of conflicting goals of management was the sales of the subsidiary. High levels of sales were postulated to provide greater potential for conflicting goals because of the importance of their size to the system. Small sales size would facilitate disinvestment, and therefore, such subsidiaries would have a greater probability of disinvestment.

$$p(D) = -2.35 \qquad -.20 \, (X6)$$
$$ (1.0) \qquad\quad (.99)$$
$$R^2 = .01$$
$$n = 2600$$

No. of disinvestments $= 140$

where $X6 = $ the levels of sales coded on five levels as explained in the assets/sales ratio with 5 representing the largest sales amount.

The regression equation shows the expected result with higher levels of sales yielding a lower probability of disinvestment. The high probability of sign indicates a high degree of confidence in the results even though the R^2 is low.

Entry Year of the Subsidiary

A third proxy for the potential for conflicting management goals is the length of time in the parent system. It was hypothesized that older subsidiaries would have developed a greater sense of identification with the system, and management would be reluctant to disinvest them.

$$p(D) = -2.26 \qquad +.005 \, (X7)$$
$$ (1.0) \qquad\quad (.91)$$
$$R^2 = .01$$
$$n = 3795$$

No. of disinvestments $= 474$

where $X7 = $ the year the subsidiary entered the system ranging from 01 representing 1901 or before to 75 for 1975.

As hypothesized, subsidiaries which had a greater length of time in the system, in which case the variable was smaller, showed a smaller probability of disinvestment. There is, however, a 9% chance that the sign of the coefficient might be negative which would mean that the opposite relationship could hold. This in conjunction with the low R^2 allows only a moderate degree of confidence in the results.

Examined individually, each of the variables showed the hypothesized relationship with the probability of disinvestment for a subsidiary. Even though the R^2's indicated that the variables explained very little of the total variance in the data base, the relatively high probability of sign for all of the variables except assets/sales ratio gives at least a moderate degree of confidence that the signs of the coefficients of the variables are as the disinvestment model hypothesized.

Multiple Regression

To examine the impact of the combined variables on the probability of disinvestment, a multiple regression was run. The variables were:

Proxies for economic justification of disinvestment
    X1—Industry concentration
    X2—Number of different products produced by the subsidiary
Proxy for interdependence
    X3—Level of intrasystem sales
Proxy for specific assets
    X4—Assets/sales ratio
Proxies for conflicting management goals
    X5—Method of entry of the subsidiary
    X6—Subsidiary sales
    X7—Entry year of the subsidiary

$$p(D) = -1.5 \quad -.002\,(X1) \quad -.12\,(X2) \quad -.65\,(X3) \quad -.08\,(X4)$$
$$ (.98) \qquad (.71) \qquad\quad (.95) \qquad\quad (1.0) \qquad\quad (.58)$$
$$ +.20\,(X5) \quad -.11\,(X6) \quad -.004\,(X7)$$
$$ (.86) \qquad\quad (.90) \qquad\quad (.72)$$

$R^2 = .02$
n $= 2600$
No. of disinvestments $= 140$

The coefficients for the variables have the impact on the probability of disinvestment as was hypothesized by the disinvestment model, with the exception of the year of entry. The probabilities of the signs do not allow a high level of confidence in the results, with the exception of the level of intrasystem sales and the number of products produced by the subsidiary.

The low R^2 means that the equation explained very little of the variance in the data. Although disappointing, the low explanatory power of the equation was not altogether surprising. Since none of the variables are direct measures of the factors hypothesized by the disinvestment model, imprecision is to be expected. In addition, the variables were not expected to explain all of the variance. As an example, the proxies for conflicting management goals examined only three of many different facets of this factor.

The results of this regression equation could be considered to provide strong support for the number of products and the level of intrasystem sales hypotheses, moderate support for the sales level hypothesis, and somewhat less support for the others. Considering the difficulties of measuring the factors used in the disinvestment model, which necessitated the use of surrogates, the strong to moderate support for several variables should not be lightly dismissed.

Perhaps one reason for the low explanatory power of the equation is the large number of observations which were eliminated because of missing data for the assets and/or sales levels. These exclusions resulted in a data base for the regressions which included these two variables of only 2,600 subsidiaries with 140 disinvestments.

To determine if this was a factor, another multiple regression was run without these two variables. This yielded the following equation.

$$p(D) = -.79 + .001(X1) - .28(X2) - 1.41(X3) + .17(X5)$$
$$(.99) \quad (.66) \qquad (1.0) \qquad (1.0) \qquad (.94)$$
$$- .004(X7)$$
$$(.78)$$

$$R^2 = .08$$
$$n = 3665$$

No. of disinvestments = 444

The results of this regression show additional explanatory power, i.e., higher R^2; however, the sign changed on the coefficient for X1, the industry concentration level. The probability of the sign remained low, however. In addition, the sign for the entry year continued to differ from the hypothesized relationship, but, again, the probability of the sign is not very high.

Thus, for these two variables, the results are somewhat uncertain. The other three variables in the model—number of products, intrasystem sales, and method of entry—continued to be supported by the regression results.

A summary of all of the regression equations is shown in Table 4-1.

IV. Summary

In order to test the hypotheses of the disinvestment model, several proxy variables were used as surrogates for the factors included in the model.

$$p(D) = f(CF, k, I, SA, CMG)$$

The variables used were:

X1—Industry concentration
X2—Number of products produced by the subsidiary
X3—Level of intrasystem sales
X4—Assets/sales ratio

Table 4-1

Summary of Logistic Regression Equations

Variable	Regression Coefficients								
	#1	#2	#3	#4	#5	#6	#7	#8	#9
β_0	-1.80 (1.0)	-1.40 (1.0)	-1.30 (1.0)	-2.80 (1.0)	-2.99 (1.0)	-2.35 (1.0)	-2.26 (1.0)	-1.50 (.98)	-.79 (.99)
X1—Industry Concentration	-.003 (.89)								.001 (.66)
X2—Number of Products		-.33 (1.0)						-.12 (.95)	-.28 (1.0)
X3—Intrasystem Sales			-1.40 (1.0)					-.65 (1.0)	-1.41 (1.0)
X4—Assets/Sales Ratio				-.05 (.55)				-.08 (.58)	
X5—Acquisition Dummy					.26 (.93)			.20 (.86)	.17 (.94)
X6—Subsidiary Sales						-.20 (.99)		-.11 (.90)	
X7—Entry Year							.005 (.91)	-.004 (.72)	-.004 (.78)
R^2	.01	.02	.08	.01	.01	.01	.01	.02	.08
n	3795	3795	3665	2600	3665	2600	3795	2600	3665
No. of Disinvestments	474	474	444	140	444	140	474	140	444

X5—Entry method for the subsidiary
X6—Sales level for the subsidiary
X7—Entry year for the subsidiary

The variables were utilized in a series of logistic regressions run on the subsidiaries included in the Harvard Multinational Enterprise Study. This data base was adjusted to exclude factors not included in the scope of the study.

Two of the variables, the number of products and the level of intrasystem sales, both showed strong results with probabilities of sign of 1.0 indicating a very high probability that the sign of the variable was correct. Both also showed the hypothesized negative effect on disinvestment. Those subsidiaries which entered the system by acquisition were shown to be more likely to be disinvested, as was hypothesized, although the probability of sign was not as high, about 90%.

The results for the sales level also were correctly signed at a 90% or better probability of sign. This suggests that as hypothesized, large subsidiaries, as measured by sales, are less likely to be disinvested.

Thus, a subsidiary that sells little of its output to other members of the multinational system, that makes only a few products, that is relatively small, and that was acquired is more likely to be disinvested than a subsidiary that sells much of its output to other members of the system, makes many products, is relatively large, and was newly formed by the parent company.

The other three variables, industry concentration, asset/sales ratio, and entry year were not supported by the results. These variables all showed low probabilities of sign and in some cases signs which were the opposite of the hypothesized relationships.

5

The Role of Facilitating Factors in Disinvestment

The model of disinvestment which has been developed suggests that for disinvestment to occur it must be economically justified. However, the model also states that disinvestments may not occur when justified, because of conflicting management goals or management barriers. Therefore, in order for disinvestment to take place, it may be necessary for some other factors to overcome these management barriers to disinvestment.

In physical terms, the law of inertia states that it requires a much larger force to move an object from a stationary position than to keep it moving once it has begun. Applied to a corporate system, it can be postulated that some force must be applied to move it from the steady state and carry out needed changes. The economic factors which justify disinvestment are necessary conditions; disinvestment is not likely to occur if there is no economic rationale to support it. However, the economics of the situation are not always sufficient in overcoming the barriers; therefore other forces or stimuli may be required.

I. Possible Disinvestment Facilitators

The concept of management barriers suggests that one possible factor which could facilitate disinvestment is a change in management. If a company has not disinvested subsidiaries because of managerial barriers, a change in management might eliminate this problem.[1] A new management might want to disinvest poorly performing subsidiaries to demonstrate an ability to deal with difficult problems, to show an immediate affect on corporate performance, or to demonstrate that they are in control. The disinvestment of subsidiaries by a new management is also facilitated by the opportunity to blame the poor performance of the disinvested subsidiaries on the predecessor management, and by the lack of identification with the subsidiary.

A commonly used instrument to gauge the performance of a management team is the earnings of the company. So long as the earnings of a system are satisfactory, management will be judged as performing well. If the earnings become less than satisfactory, it will be believed that management is performing poorly. The market indicator of system performance, the stock price, reflects both the confidence investors have in the management and the level of earnings in the company.

Since management must therefore be concerned about the earnings performance of the system, each subsidiary should be contributing to the overall earnings. However, as long as other subsidiaries within the system are doing well, management may not be too concerned about the impact of a poor performer. Its minimal contribution can be hidden by the performance of the other subsidiaries. Management can avoid disinvesting the poorly performing subsidiaries as long as other subsidiaries generate a sufficiently high level of profits.

However, when the earnings performance of the system becomes less than satisfactory, management will not be able to hide the marginal subsidiaries. This suggests that another possible contributing factor for disinvestment is a decrease in the earnings of the system. When this occurs, management may want to disinvest the poorly performing subsidiaries so that they will not be a drag on the system's performance. This might improve the earnings and enhance a return to a satisfactory level.

An additional argument for an increased occurence of disinvestment during times of poor earnings performance can be made on the basis of capital needs. If new investments are required to restore the profitability of the system, the company may have difficulty raising the needed funds. The traditional sources of capital, debt and equity, might be closed off or prohibitively expensive because of the increased risk caused by the declining earnings of the system. Therefore, the company might look to disinvestments of subsidiaries as a means of raising needed capital.

There are, of course, other indicators of financial performance which could be used. Return on sales and return on investment are two measures which are commonly used for internal reporting purposes. The use of earnings, however, has additional appeal as it is regularly used by investors in evaluating the market prices of stock and burden coverage for debt.

It is, therefore, hypothesized that two factors which could serve as stimuli to overcome the barriers to disinvestment are: (1) change in management and (2) decrease in system earnings.

The reaction to either of these factors, however, may not be immediate. A new management team may need to review the performance of subsidiaries before deciding on disinvestment. Management might be tempted to try other methods of improving earnings performance in the system before resolving to disinvest some of the poorer performers. These considerations indicate that there might be a lag between the occurrence of these stimuli and the resultant impact on disinvestment. This means that the precise timing of the effect cannot be accurately predicted, although the effect itself may be.

II. The Data Base for Testing the Facilitating Factors

To test whether these two conditions are contributing factors or facilitators of disinvestment, the data base used in the previous chapter was utilized with two major modifications.

In the data base used in the previous chapter, only those subsidiaries in industries which had had disinvestments were included. This was because of uncertainty whether disinvestment was warranted or possible in those industries with no disinvestments.

For these tests a somewhat similar exclusion was made; those systems which did not make at least one disinvestment during the period were excluded. This exclusion was based again on the uncertainty concerning the feasibility of the disinvestment alternative in those systems where no disinvestments were made. In addition, since the purpose of these tests was to determine the existence of factors which facilitated disinvestment, there needed to have been disinvestment to facilitate.

This adjustment resulted in 18 companies being excluded for not having made any disinvestments between 1968 and 1975. Another 13 companies were excluded because of incomplete data. This left a total of 156 parent systems for the analysis.

The other modification of the data base resulted from the change in the orientation of the tests. In the previous chapter, various characteristics of subsidiaries were tested to determine their impact on the probability of the subsidiary's disinvestment. For the tests for contributing factors, however, · timing of the disinvestment was the primary concern.

The best method to have tested these factors would have been to have had an observation for each subsidiary for each year. This approach would have allowed a combination of the variables used in the previous chapter with the additional variables for changes in management and a decrease in earnings. However, the Harvard Multinational Enterprise Study did not include information for each subsidiary for each year, but only a single observation for the year of disinvestment or for 1975, the last year included in the study.

Thus, rather than having a separate observation for each subsidiary, the observations were for each year for each system. As an example, there was an observation for the year 1968 for system A. Included in this observation were the data on the number of subsidiaries which were disinvested during that year by that system. The next observation included the number of subsidiaries which were disinvested by system A in 1969, and so forth.

III. The Variables

Disinvestment as Related to Changes in Management

For each parent system, it was determined for each year whether a change in the Chief Executive Officer (CEO) or the apparent "second in command," termed the Chief Operating Officer (COO) in most companies, had occurred. The top two officers in the companies were selected because this information was readily available through annual reports. It was very difficult to determine the relative rankings of lower levels of officers and, therefore, only the top two were used. Also, to allow for time lags, changes in 1965, 1966, and 1967 were included. In coding these changes, a dummy variable of "1" was used to indicate a change and "0" to indicate no change.

It was hypothesized that a change in management would facilitate disinvestment. Thus one would expect an increase in disinvestments following a change in management.

It was also suggested that the timing of the impact of a change in management was uncertain. A change in one year might not result in disinvestments until the following or even subsequent years. To allow for this, the two variables, representing changes in the CEO and COO, were each lagged for periods of 1 and 2 years. This resulted in two series of 3 variables representing changes in the CEO and COO.

Disinvestment as Related to a Decrease in System Earnings

The net income data for each of the parent systems for each year was determined including 1964-1967. To indicate a decrease in earnings, a dummy variable was created which was coded "1" if the net income decreased from the previous year or "0" if the net income remained constant or increased.

Data on earnings per share was also collected. As was to be expected, the pattern of net income per share followed the total net income. Since the two measures proved to be essentially the same, only the total net income variable was used in the tests.

Since it was hypothesized that falling earnings would be a contributing factor for disinvestment, one would expect an increase in disinvestment occurring after a fall in earnings.

As with the changes in management, the timing of the impact of a decrease in earnings was not clear. Thus, the variable representing a decrease in earnings was also lagged for the 1 and 2 year periods, resulting in a series of 3 variables indicating a decrease in system net income.

Correlation of Variables

One of the concerns about using the variables for management changes and reduction in system earnings is that both could be indicating the same condition. One could suspect that if the system earnings were to decrease a change in top management of the system could occur. Thus the use of one set of variables would accomplish the same test as using both.

To determine whether these variables were correlated, the correlation matrix shown in Table 5-1 was developed. The variables for a change in CEO and COO were included as were the variables for decreases in system earnings. The lagged variables for the system earnings reductions were included since a change in management might not occur the same year as the earnings reduction occurred. A change which was related to the fall in earnings might not take place until subsequent years.

Examining Table 5-1 indicates that changes in CEO and COO are somewhat correlated as would be expected. However, the correlations between the management changes and the variables representing earnings decreases are so small that they are insignificant.

IV. Test Results

To test the variables for each year in which disinvestment occurred within a parent system, a dummy variable was coded as "1." If disinvestment did not occur, the dummy variable was coded "0." This dummy variable indicating whether disinvestment occurred in a given system in a given year was used as the dependent variable in a logistic regression analysis.

The use of the lagged variables reduced the number of years of data available for each system to seven. This resulted in 1092 observations, 7 years for each of the 156 companies. Of this group of potential occurrences, disinvestment took place in 178 observations.

Change in the Chief Executive Officer

The regression runs using the independent variable representing a change in the chief executive officer are shown on Table 5-2. It was hypothesized that a change in the CEO would facilitate disinvestment of subsidiaries, and therefore, one would expect that the coefficient of the variable would be positive.

The regression results indicated that the coefficient was incorrectly signed for one of the three variables related to a change in CEO, a change in the same year as the disinvestment. The other two variables, lags of one and two years, were all positively signed as expected. The combination of all of the variables

Disinvestment of Foreign Subsidiaries

Table 5-1

Correlation Matrix

Variable	1	2	3	4	5
1 Change in Chief Executive Officer	1.0				
2 Change in Chief Operating Officer	.42*	1.0			
3 Decrease in Net Income—Year 0	.03	.04	1.0		
4 Decrease in Net Income—Lag 1 year	.02	.00	.09	1.0	
5 Decrease in Net income—Lag 2 years	.01	.00	− .13	.08	1.0

*Statistically significant at better than the .01 level. Others not statistically significant.

Table 5-2

**Logistic Regressions for
Change in Chief Executive Officer (CEO)**

Variable	#1	#2	#3	#4
		Regression Equations		
β_0	−1.63 (1.0)*	−1.65 (1.0)	−1.64 (1.0)	−1.64 (1.0)
Change in CEO— Year 0	−.11 (.65)			−.09 (.63)
Change in CEO—Lag 1 year		.17 (.74)		.15 (.72)
Change in CEO—Lag 2 years			−.02 (.53)	−.02 (.53)
R^2	.00	.00	.00	.01
n	1092	1092	1092	1092
No. of Disinvestments	178	178	178	178

*probability of sign

yielded signs which were unchanged from the regressions using each variable individually.

The probabilities of the signs for all of the variables were quite low. This coupled with the fact that two of the variables were signed contrary to the hypothesis and the low R^2 suggests that the results should be considered as not supporting the hypothesis.

Change in the Chief Operating Officer

The regression results for change in the chief operating officer are shown in Table 5-3. Again, the hypothesis was that a change would facilitate disinvestment. It was expected, therefore, that the sign of the coefficient for the variable would be positive.

The results suggest that, other things being equal, a change in the chief operating officer of a multinational enterprise increases the likelihood that a disinvestment of a subsidiary will occur in the following year. On the other hand, a change in the chief operating officer seemed to have no significant effect on the likelihood of a disinvestment either during the year of the change or 2 years later.

Decrease in System Earnings

Table 5-4 gives the results of the regression runs using the variable representing a decrease in the parent system earnings. The hypothesis for this variable was that a decrease in earnings would contribute to disinvestment. This would indicate that the sign of the coefficient for the variable would be positive.

An examination of the data in Table 5-4 indicates that although all of the variables for a reduction in system earnings were signed as expected, the one year lag provided the best results. The low probabilities of signs for the other two variables make their results almost meaningless.

The results for the decrease in system earnings are, therefore, similar to the change in the chief operating officer with the one year lag showing the best results.

Combinations of Variables

To determine whether the management and net income factors in combination showed an effect on the disinvestment occurrence, two additional regressions were run. The first, shown in Table 5-5, combined the one variable from each of the three categories which had shown the best relationship to disinvestment as measured by the probability of sign in the previous regressions. The second regressions, Table 5-6, combined all of the variables.

Table 5-3

**Logistic Regressions for
Change in Chief Operating Officer (COO)**

Variable	#1	#2	#3	#4
		Regression Equations		
β_0	−1.65 (1.0)	−1.71 (1.0)	−1.62 (1.0)	−1.76 (1.0)
Change in COO— Year 0	.10 (.67)			.14 (.74)
Change in COO— Lag 1 year		.43 (.98)		.44 (.98)
Change in COO— Lag 2 years			−.14 (.72)	−.08 (.64)
R^2	.00	.01	.00	.01
n	1092	1092	1092	1092
No. of Disinvestments	178	178	178	178

Table 5-4

Logistic Regressions for Decrease in System Net Income (NI)

| | Regression Equations | | | |
Variable	#1	#2	#3	#4
β_0	− 1.66 (1.0)	− 1.71 (1.0)	− 1.65 (1.0)	− 1.87 (1.0)
Decrease in NI— Year 0	.09 (.69)			.03 (.57)
Decrease in NI— Lag 1 year		.25 (.92)		.24 (.91)
Decrease in NI— Lag 2 years			.03 (.56)	.04 (.58)
R_2	.00	.01	.00	.01
n	1092	1092	1092	1092
No. of Disinvestments	178	178	178	178

Table 5-5

Logistic Regressions for Best Individual Variables

Variable	Regression Coefficients
β_0	-1.77
	(1.0)
Change in CEO—Lag 1 year	$-.09$
	$(.62)$
Change in COO—Lag 1 year	$.44$
	$(.97)$
Decrease in NI—Lag 1 year	$.23$
	$(.91)$
R^2	$.01$
n	1092
No. of Disinvestments	178

Table 5-6

Multiple Logistic Regression for All Variables

Variable	Regression Coefficients	
β_0	-1.95	$(1.0)^*$
Change in CEO—Year 0	$-.20$	$(.74)$
Change in CEO—Lag 1 year	$-.08$	$(.61)$
Change in CEO—Lag 2 years	$.09$	$(.61)$
Change in COO—Year 0	$.18$	$(.78)$
Change in COO—Lag 1 year	$.44$	$(.97)$
Change in COO—Lag 2 years	$-.13$	$(.69)$
Decrease in NI—Year 0	$.05$	$(.62)$
Decrease in NI—Lag 1 year	$.22$	$(.89)$
Decrease in NI—Lag 2 years	$.04$	$(.58)$
R^2	$.02$	
n	1092	
No. of Disinvestments	178	

*probability of sign

Both tables showed similar results. The variables that were important on the simple regressions—a one year lag for a change in the COO and a one year lag for a decline in system profits—continued to be important in the multiple regression. This result is reasonable as management is likely to act quickly if they are going to disinvest. As with the simple regression model, the change in CEO was not important in the multiple regression model.

The usefulness of the multiple regression approach is that it allows the other variables to be held constant and the impact of each individual variable to be determined. The two multiple regressions, however, showed no significant changes from the simple regressions. The R^2 was still low and the coefficients and probabilities of sign for the variables were essentially unchanged.

Although the R^2 improved with this approach, it was still very low. This low R^2 could have occurred for several reasons.

The regression analysis does provide support for the hypothesis that changes in management and falling system earnings facilitate or contribute to disinvestment decisions. In addition to these, there may be other facilitating factors or conditions. The existence of other factors could be one reason for the low explanatory power of the three variables which were tested.

In addition to a change in the chief operating officer and a decline in system earnings, other factors not included in these equations could also have significant impact on the disinvestment decisions. The factors discussed in Chapter 4 and other factors such as anti-trust activities, tax law changes, a general economic downturn, political instability, repatriation limitations, and exchange rate and foreign exchange controls could all contribute to disinvestment decisions.

As previously noted, changes in management and a decrease in system earnings are suggested to facilitate disinvestment when such is otherwise appropriate. If disinvestment is not justified, then it is unlikely that these factors would cause disinvestment to take place. Because of the difficulties of examining from an external position the internal analysis concerning cash flows and discount rates, it was not possible to identify precisely which subsidiaries should have been disinvested. Thus, if one of these factors occurred when no disinvestments were economically justified, then of course disinvestment was not likely to have occurred. This problem was undoubtedly a contributant to the low R^2 for the regressions.

V. Summary

It was proposed that disinvestments might not occur when economically justified because of management's resistance to disinvestment. This resistance, termed a barrier to disinvestment, might be overcome by other factors which would facilitate or contribute to the disinvestment decisions. Two possible disinvestment stimuli were suggested, a change in top level management and a decrease in the parent system earnings.

Using the data from the Harvard Multinational Enterprise study data base, the impact of three sets of variables on disinvestment occurrence were tested. The three groups, change in the chief executive officer, change in the chief operating officer, and a decrease in the net income of the system, included lagged variables to examine whether the disinvestment decisions lagged the occurrence of these conditions.

Using the logistic regression function, the tests of the variables produced mixed results. The impact of a change in the CEO was uncertain as the signs of the coefficients of the variables fluctuated. A change in chief operating officer was moderately related to disinvestment one year later. A decrease in system earnings similarly was related to disinvestment one year later. The other time lags for these two variables did not produce any significant results.

6

Disinvestment Case Studies

The examination of the disinvestment activity on an aggregative basis does not allow for a complete understanding of the factors affecting disinvestment decisions. The data based on company and industry totals may provide some support for disinvestment patterns based on underlying economic situations. However, the individual management in each given situation is required to make the decision of whether to disinvest or not.

As previously noted, managerial motivations, concerns, and/or problems will have an impact on the disinvestment activity. The role of these factors can only be ascertained on an individual basis by means of case studies.

In an attempt to locate case studies for development and inclusion in this study, approximately 45 companies were contacted. According to various magazines and journals, each of these companies had recently disinvested at least one subsidiary. Of these companies, only two allowed a review of disinvestment situations.

Unfortunately, one of the available situations, American Machinery, proved to be a disinvestment of a joint venture. Although joint ventures were excluded in the preceding data analysis, this particular case was thought to provide insights into the disinvestment process and was therefore included.

After the description of the two cases, a comparison of the cases to the hypothesized disinvestment model is included in the summary.

I. American Standard

In 1971, a new management team took control at American Standard. They undertook a review of all company operations with the objective of improving liquidity and long-term profitability. The general strategy was to examine the industry prospects for each of American Standard's businesses without regard to foreign versus domestic operations. The industries were evaluated on how they matched American Standard's goals rather than how well the foreign or domestic subsidiary was performing.

In the study of the heating business, management discovered some basic problems. Long a mainstay of American Standard's operations, the industry had undergone a change. In the United States the industry was moving away from the traditional wet heat operations (radiators) toward forced air, and in Europe demand was shifting to steel radiator products from American Standard's cast iron. These two trends combined to move the market away from American Standard's strengths. Whereas American Standard's expertise was in higher technology and capital intensive production, the demand was moving toward labor intensive products. This resulted in many firms entering the market, severe competition, and falling profit margins. The associated overcapacity in the cast iron industry also contributed to decreasing profits.

After analyzing these developments, top-level corporate management believed that the long-term prospects for the heating business were bleak and that American Standard could compete better in other markets. However, the operating group managements in the U.S. and Europe who were responsible for the heating business disagreed with this decision. Both groups believed that the heating business still had long-term profit potential and neither wanted to disinvest their heating operations. The European management was particularly adamant about retaining this business.

The heating business was very important in the European group, contributing $200 million of a total of $400 million in annual sales. In addition, a new European group manager had been installed, and he as well as the country managing directors were anxious to demonstrate their abilities. They argued that this major business and American Standards' large market positions could be made viable if properly managed. This would call for rationalization of facilities, models, etc. Corporate management, willing to be shown and not wishing to demoralize the group manager and his key people, decided to allow them some time to improve the heating operations.

The most important segment of American Standard's European heating sales was provided by the French subsidiary, Ideal Standard France. Although some other product lines were included in its operations, most of its sales were of heating products. Buoyed by strong markets, the subsidiary had the best year in its 80-year history in 1973, $110 million in sales and $10 million in profits. To maintain this trend, European group management commenced a program of about $6 million to rationalize and modernize in particular the Belgian and French facilities.

When the building industry in general declined in 1974, the European group manager recognized that some additional measures would need to be taken in order to continue the profits of the previous year. Questioning the ability of the incumbent country manager to take the austerity measures which were called for, the group manager departed from the traditional policy of having nationals manage the subsidiaries and installed in the spring of 1974 an Englishman who had a good record in the company.

Following the traditional summer vacation month, the new manager was able to complete a review of the subsidiary's operations. He discovered that the subsidiary was losing about $1 million per month and the bank debt, which had been negligible at the beginning of the year, had increased to over $8 million. In reporting this to group management, he indicated that this was probably caused by the general recession, credit restrictions, and price controls.

The losses continued into the fall, and group and corporate management personnel held a series of tense meetings in Paris in late 1974. The conclusion of these meetings was that the only way to stop the losses was to reduce the labor force and close 4 of the 6 plants. The subsidiary manager immediately commenced negotiations with the French government authorities for permission to take these steps.

In February of 1975, the government authorized the lay-off of the workers, which the subsidiary did at a cost of $4 million in severance pay. The government, however, refused to allow the closing of the plants, although they did grant some relief from the price controls.

These concessions were not sufficient. The subsidiary continued to lose money, and by the beginning of the summer of 1975, bank debt had grown to $17 million with an additional $5 million advanced by the parent company plus a $5 sale-leaseback arrangement with the banks. The net worth of the subsidiary had dropped from $33 million at the end of 1973 to about $17 million.

Group management had continued to meet with corporate management, and by this time both management groups agreed that the business was fundamentally bad and that the rewards for continued operations were not commensurate with the risks. Together they decided to put Ideal Standard France into a form of receivership. Although the accumulated bank debt of the subsidiary had not been guaranteed by the parent company, it was thought that there were sufficient assets in the subsidiary for the creditors to recover their funds.

After the disinvestment of the French company, the largest of the subsidiaries in the heating business, and with a general disenchantment as to the long term outlook for the industry, it did not seem reasonable to continue to operate the smaller European units. Subsequently, the German heating oeprations were shut down in early 1976; the profitable Austrian and British operations—along with the unprofitable Belgian heating business—was sold for about book value to a British company; and the Swiss subsidiary, which was modestly profitable, was sold to a Swiss company in March 1977 for approximately book value. Unable to find a buyer for the Italian subsidiary, American Standard continued to operate the subsidiary until 1978 when it was finally sold.

II. American Machinery, Inc.

American Machinery, Inc. (AMI), a major U.S. company, was the sole owner of an Australian subsidiary, Australian Climax Ltd. In the early 1960s,

Australian Climax was merged with Commercial Products, a subsidiary of Cannon, Ltd. a large diversified Australian company with primarily consumer products, to form a 50-50 joint venture called Australian Climax Commercial (ACC). This jointly owned firm produced a large variety of products, primarily heavy machinery including machine tools such as riveting machines, stamping presses, turret lathes, and textile machinery.

In the mid-sixties, following a change in management, ACC decided that many of its small volume businesses were not contributing to ACC's profits, and their elimination was commenced. This disinvestment of the small operations took until the middle of 1970.

Concurrent with this activity, a small management team was appointed to determine a long range strategy for ACC. Since earnings could not support investment in all areas, the study was to recommend the required rationalization.

After several months of preparation, the final presentation was completed in the spring of 1972. The report examined the profit and sales potential of all business areas, reviewed U.S. plans, and described management capabilities. The team developed a priority listing of the different ACC businesses. In this listing, textile machinery occupied the lowest priority. However, prior to the study's completion, the status of textile machinery was clear, and the management team had commenced an in-depth study of the business which was completed by mid-1972. The team concluded that although the textile machinery operations were profitable, ACC did not have funds for the required continuing investment in the operation because other product lines were more important in the long range plans of ACC and were more in the mainstream of AMI strategy.

The in-depth study included an analysis of ACC's options, including disinvestment. However, since ACC management knew of no potential buyers, they concluded that selling the business was not the solution. The end result of the study was an indication that textile machinery was questionable in ACC's future but uncertainty about what to do with it.

At the same time that these events were occurring at ACC, the Vice President for AMI-Asia received an assignment to review the existing product lines in Asia and to examine rationalization possibilities. One reason for the review was corporate management's belief that the ratios of employees to sales in Asia, and especially in Australia, were out of line with the corporate pattern. The status as of 1970 was as follows:

	Australia	Asia	US
Sales (millions)	$100	$250	$2600
Employees (thousands)	10	14	45
Sales per Employee (thousand)	$10	$18	$58

As part of this review, it was decided that 100% ownership of ACC would be best for AMI. This would facilitate taking the action necessary to bring about the desired productivity improvements in ACC. Therefore, beginning in 1969, AMI-Asia began to mention in the regular quarterly meetings with the management of Cannon, Ltd. a willingness to purchase their 50% interest in ACC. Cannon was not opposed to this idea, but their suggested selling price was too high for AMI.

During this period, Cannon had become disenchanted with its diversification into industrial products. They had begun to disinvest their industrial holdings in order to concentrate more on their traditional strengths in consumer products. This concern was heightened by the 1970-1971 recession which depressed ACC's as well as Cannon's earnings.

During the 1972 fourth quarter meeting, Cannon mentioned that they had been informally approached by Bamberger Industrial Equipment, a local company involved in manufacturing and distributing industrial machinery. Bamberger had learned of Cannon's displeasure with their diversified holdings and had offered to purchase their half of ACC. However, according to the original merger agreement, any sale of equity in ACC was subject to the approval of the other joint partner, and AMI did not agree to the sale to Bamberger. They had been happy with Cannon as a partner; Cannon had been passive in their operations of ACC but very active in financing activities. AMI was concerned that the overlapping interests of Bamberger would necessitate additional top level management involvement—a situation that AMI wished to avoid.

AMI, therefore, made a counter suggestion to Cannon. They proposed acquiring Cannon's ACC shares and subsequently negotiating separately with Bamberger to sell some of ACC's businesses. This proposal was acceptable to Cannon management.

In the summer of 1972, the president of AMI-Asia made direct contact with the joint managing director of Bamberger to explore the possibility of selling parts of ACC to them, particularly the textile machinery business. Bamberger expressed interest in such a purchase.

Following these preliminary discussions with Bamberger, the president of AMI-Asia went to New York to present the proposal to AMI management. Seeing this as an opportunity to achieve the desired 100% ownership of ACC with a minimum cost to the corporation, corporate management approved the plan.

Two separate negotiations then commenced. AMI-Asia management met with Cannon to assess a value for ACC and to determine what Cannon wanted for their 50% share. Management of both AMI-Asia and ACC met with Bamberger to discuss what businesses to include in the sale and the appropriate price.

The negotiations with Cannon proceeded very smoothly and rapidly.

Basically, Cannon received the price they requested. They proposed that they be paid the amount of their original investment plus a return on the investment. AMI-Asia believed that this represented only a modest return and agreed to the price. The most difficult part of this arrangement was to convince AMI management in New York of the reasonableness of the price. Since the payment to Cannon had to be made before the sale to Bamberger was completed, AMI management was concerned about the cash outflow. However, they agreed to the price proposed by Cannon and AMI-Asia, and the payment was made to complete the purchase of the equity in the summer of 1973. The purchase price was about 25% above the book value of the equity.

The negotiations with Bamberger took some additional time. Initially ACC proposed that two businesses be sold: the textile machinery operation and consumer hand tools. The textile machinery business was operating profitably and the consumer hand tools were marginally profitable.

It became obvious after the initial negotiating session that Bamberger was most interested in the textile machinery operations and was placing little value on the hand tools business. Already active in industrial machinery distribution, they were very eager to expand their growing manufacturing operations, which the purchase of ACC's textile machinery business would allow them to do.

In preparing for the second negotiation meeting, ACC decided to propose selling only the textile machinery business. This represented about $14 million in sales and 1,500 employees. In considering what price to ask, ACC management evaluated three different approaches:

1. Previous net income times a multiplier (last three years times 10).
2. Projections of future cash flow and calculation of net present value (used ACC cost of capital).
3. Forecast of replacement cost and cost of new entry.

In the second meeting, ACC proposed selling only the textile machinery business. Bamberger immediately agreed to this. In presenting their proposed selling price, ACC management emphasized the high cost of entering the business as well as the problems that the existing oligopolists would cause a new manufacturer. With this introduction, they indicated what they considered to be a fair price. This proved to be about equal to the NPV calculation, although all three approaches were considered. It was about 1/2 of the replacement cost but significantly higher than the last three years income times 10. Bamberger accepted the price without any further negotiation.

Because of ACC's previous experiences with smaller disinvestments, management was able to complete the negotiations with a minimum of difficulty. This previous experience was particularly helpful in negotiating the price and the allocation of the selling price between assets and goodwill. The sale to Bamberger was completed in the fall of 1973.

III. Summary

It is useful to compare these case studies with the variables of the disinvestment model as a method of determining whether these disinvestments occurred as prescribed.

Cash Flows and Discount Rate

The analysis of the American Standard subsidiary included an examination of the cash flows. Several years before the disinvestment actually occurred, corporate management foresaw a reduction in cash flows from the heating business and recommended disinvestment at that time. Just prior to the disinvestment, the subsidiary suffered from severe cash problems and was forced to borrow to finance its operations.

The textile operations of Australian Climax Commercial, on the other hand, were operating profitably and were expected to continue to provide a satisfactory cash flow. In this case, the problem was that other operations were expected to provide higher cash flows, and therefore, the opportunity cost of investments in textiles was quite high. This resulted in the present value of the textile operation falling in relation to other product lines.

Both of these empirical studies supported the cash flow and discount rate hypothesis of the disinvestment model, although the statistical tests in Chapter 4 using proxy variables were inconclusive.

Interdependence

Neither of the subsidiaries which were disinvested had significant amounts of sales to other activities within the parent system. This is in accordance with the disinvestment model.

Beyond this particular variable, however, it is important to note that both of these subsidiaries were quite independent of other activities within the system. The textile operations of ACC, in fact, were physically separate. Neither operation was an important consumer of intermediate products manufactured elsewhere in the system nor were there any shared production facilities. Each operated relatively independently in distributing and marketing its products.

Specific Assets

Although the production process in both cases required specialized machinery, these machines were readily transferable to the new owners without loss of earnings potential. Both subsidiaries had recognizable tradenames, but this did not seem to be a deterrent. The purchaser of ACC's textile operations,

Bamberger, had their own tradename, while Ideal Standard France operated in a market where tradename was not very important.

Thus, in neither of these cases were specific assets a hindrance to disinvestment. However, since the assets/sales ratios for these subsidiaries were not available for comparison to the data used in the statistical tests, no conclusions as to the variable used in the statistical tests in Chapter 4 could be drawn.

Conflicting Management Goals

Conflicting management goals seemed to have the most impact in the American Standard case. The original disinvestment decision was made several years before the subsidiary was finally disinvested. Australian Climax Commercial had undertaken a study of the textile operations, recognizing the problem situation, but disinvestment was not considered initially.

None of the variables used in testing the model in regard to conflicting management goals seemed to be an explicit concern with either of these disinvestments. Although the case studies do not provide sufficient information to examine what the conflicting goals might have been, the delays in both cases between the recognition of the problem and the actual disinvestment suggest that some conflicts may have existed.

In neither case did a fall in corporate earnings seem to be a contributing factor as a disinvestment stimulus. A change in management did provide a significant stimulus in the American Standard decision to disinvest its subsidiary. In addition, external stimuli, a purchase offer in the case of ACC and a recession for American Standard, were important in both cases in facilitating the disinvestment process.

The case studies supported some of the concepts of the disinvestment model, if not the specific variables used in the data analysis in previous chapters. While no conclusions could be drawn for the specific assets factor, the cash flow, discount rate, interdependence, and conflicting management goals were supported.

It may be important to note that in locating these two case studies, companies were contacted only after determining from public records that they had disinvested a subsidiary. Only three companies were willing to discuss their disinvestments—the two cases included and another which was not included because the disinvestment occurred following government pressures. In some cases, the companies denied having made any disinvestments. Although certainly not a "statistically significant" finding, the lack of cooperation supports the suggestion that companies treat disinvestments as failures rather than normal proceedings of business.

7

Summary

An examination of the flow and stock of foreign subsidiaries of U.S. multinational companies indicated that disinvestments of subsidiaries were increasing in significance during the late 1960s and early 1970s. To develop a model for this disinvestment activity, various theories of foreign direct investment were examined under the assumption that disinvestments were related to the factors which caused or supported the initial investment decision.

Two general categories of investments were identified: active investment to exploit a competitive advantage, and reactive investment to maintain industry stability. For both of these situations, it was suggested that disinvestment would occur when the reasons for the initial investment were no longer met. This means that for active investments, disinvestment is more likely as the competitive advantages are eroded. For those subsidiaries established for reactive reasons, the likelihood of disinvestment increases as the nature of the industry structure changes. It was therefore hypothesized that over time changes would occur which would reduce the value of the subsidiary to the parent system, increase the value of the subsidiary to a potential buyer, or a combination of both effects. When the disinvestment value exceeds the value of the subsidiary to the parent, disinvestment was hypothesized as being economically justified.

The cash flow framework was proposed for examining this situation. The value of the subsidiary was suggested to be the present value of the cash flows associated with the subsidiary discounted by the cost of capital or discount rate for the subsidiary. As changing competitive conditions or industry structures occurred, the relevant cash flows of the subsidiary could be reduced for the parent, or the discount rate could be increased. This would reduce the value to the parent while the same factors could work to increase the value to a buyer. This would result in an increased disinvestment value and a reduced retention value.

It was further hypothesized that disinvestment might not occur in these situations because of barriers to disinvestment. These barriers could be economic factors such as specificity of the subsidiaries' assets which would reduce their value to another owner or interdependence of the subsidiary with other elements of the system which would hinder the isolation of the relevant cash flows. Another type of barrier was also hypothesized: managements' reluctance to make disinvestment decisions. This reticence was attributed primarily to conflicting goals within management.

Expressing the probability of a subsidiary's disinvestment as a function of these factors, the following formulation was hypothesized:

$$p(D) = f(CF, k, I, SA, CMG)$$

Where:

p (D)	=	Probability of disinvestment of the subsidiary
CF	=	Expected future cash flows associated with the subsidiary
k	=	Discount rate for the subsidiary
I	=	Interdependence of subsidiary with system
SA	=	Level of specific assets in the subsidiary
CMG	=	Existence of conflicting goals within the management system

The managerial barrier to disinvestment hypothesis suggested that the parent might not disinvest a subsidiary when economically justified. It was posited that other factors might be needed to facilitate the disinvestment process. Two factors which could act as stimuli for the disinvestment process were suggested: a change in top management and a decrease in system earnings.

I. Findings of the Study

To determine the impact of these factors on disinvestment, variables were identified which could be used as proxies for the various factors. This was done since the factors themselves could not be directly measured with the available data bases, which were taken primarily from the Harvard Multinational Enterprise Study. The variables used in the analysis to represent the factors were:

Cash Flow and Discount Rate
> Industry concentration for subsidiary
> Number of products produced by the subsidiary

Interdependence
> Level of intrasystem sales by the subsidiary

Specific Assets
> Assets/sales ratio for the subsidiary

Conflicting Management Goals
> Entry method for the subsidiary
> Sales level for the subsidiary
> Entry year for the subsidiary

Disinvestment Stimuli
    Change in system Chief Executive Officer (CEO)
    Change in system Chief Operating Officer (COO)
    Decrease in system earnings

The variables were used in a series of logistic regression analyses to test their relationships with disinvestment. In addition, two case studies of disinvestment were examined to provide some empirical evidence on the hypothesized relationships. Table 7-1 is a summary of the results of these analyses.

The statistical tests resulted in strong support for two of the variables. As hypothesized, subsidiaries with a diversified product base, as indicated by the number of SIC product codes, were less likely to be disinvested. Subsidiaries with higher levels of interdependence, as measured by intrasystem sales, were also less likely to be disinvested.

Two of the variables used as proxies for conflicting management goals resulted in moderate support for the hypothesis. Large subsidiaries in terms of sales were less likely to be disinvested, as were subsidiaries which entered the parent system as newly formed entities.

Of the variables hypothesized as disinvestment stimuli, the change in chief operating officer and the decrease in system earnings variables with one year lags showed the best results with moderate support for the hypothesis.

The other variables used in the analysis showed inconclusive results, neither supporting nor opposing the hypotheses.

The two case studies were not very conclusive as to the specific variables used in the statistical tests. Only the changes in top management and the intrasystem sales variables were supported. However, the case studies showed that the cash flow, discount rate, and conflicting management goal factors were important even though, with the exception of the change in the chief operating officer, the specific variables used as proxies for these factors in the statistical tests were not.

II. Comparison to Other Studies

A similar type of study was undertaken by Caves and Porter[1] for domestic "businesses" of companies. These businesses were individual operations usually confined to a single 4-digit SIC category. Using a data base provided by the PIMS Program of the Strategic Planning Institute, they had access to disguised financial and market data on 556 individual businesses operated by 57 North American companies.

Their study differed from this analysis in that they focused on the characteristics of businesses which were not disinvested even though the rate of return for the business was low (assumed to be 8% or less before taxes in their study). The dependent variable in their analysis was whether a major competi-

Table 7-1

Summary of Results of Tests of Hypotheses

Variable	Hypothesized Effect on Disinvestment*	Statistical Results	Case Analysis Results
Industry Concentration	Deter	Uncertain	Uncertain
Number of Products	Deter	Strong Support	Uncertain
Intrasystem Sales	Deter	Strong Support	Supported
Assets/Sales Ratio	Deter	Uncertain	Uncertain
Acquisition Dummy	Facilitate	Moderate Support	Uncertain
Subsidiary Sales	Deter	Moderate Support	Uncertain
Entry Year	Facilitate	Uncertain	Uncertain
Change in CEO	Facilitate	Uncertain	Supported
Change in COO	Facilitate	Moderate Support**	Supported
Decrease in System Earnings	Facilitate	Moderate Support**	Uncertain

* Assuming a high value or level for the variable
** With a one year time lag

tor (5% market share or greater) in the same business exited from the market. After excluding from the sample businesses with higher rates of return and other factors which would be a disincentive to disinvest, the remaining data base consisted of 89 businesses.

Because of the access to internal financial information, they were able to specify variables which more closely corresponded to the concept of exit barriers. In addition, they were able to utilize more variables in an attempt to capture the effect of the barriers. This resulted in their regression equations having more descriptive power as defined by R^2. Nevertheless, a comparison of the results from this analysis with comparable variables from their study is interesting.

Table 7-2 shows that the major difference in the results of the two studies is the effect of intrasystem sales on the probability of disinvestment. Caves and Porter found that businesses with a higher percentage of sales within the system were more likely to be disinvested. They reasoned that businesses with a low return are likely to be suffering from production inefficiencies or inferior products. The other activities forced to purchase from that business could be placed at a disadvantage and, therefore, might provide a stimulus for management to disinvest the poorly performing business.[2]

The results of the analysis of foreign subsidiaries indicates the opposite affect—higher internal sales—leads to a lower probability of disinvestment. It was posited that subsidiaries with a higher percentage of intrasystem sales would be more interdependent with other subsidiaries. This interdependence would increase the difficulty of isolating relevant cash flows and also increase the dislocations caused by the disinvestment.

Caves and Porter used for their study only those businesses which were providing a low return. Once isolated as performing poorly, they then examined those businesses for characteristics which facilitated or deterred disinvestment.

This study included all subsidiaries, both good and poor performers, and then attempted to identify characteristics which would indicate a higher probability of disinvestment. It may be that those subsidiaries with high levels of intrasystem sales are less likely to become poor performers. With a higher level of certainty in their operations, lower marketing and perhaps distribution costs, and other considerations might allow the more integrated subsidiary to operate more profitably than an independent. If, however, the subsidiary is so inefficient as to effectively lose these advantages, then the factors which Caves and Porter described may come into consideration.

Nevertheless, there was a difference in the results with no clear-cut explanation for why this occurred.

The other differences in the results were for industry concentration, assets/sales ratio, and subsidiary time in the parent system, where this study of

Table 7-2

**Comparison of Results with Caves and Porter
Study of Domestic Disinvestment**

Variable	Effect on Disinvestment of Foreign Subsidiary	Effect on Disinvestment of Domestic Businesses[3]
Industry Concentration	Uncertain	Facilitated Disinvestment[4]
Number of Products	Deterred Disinvestment	Deterred Disinvestment[5]
Level of Intrasystem Sales	Deterred Disinvestment	Facilitated Disinvestment
Asset/Sales Ratio	Uncertain	Deterred Disinvestment
Method of Entry— Acquisition	Facilitated Disinvestment	n/a
Subsidiary Sales Level	Deterred Disinvestment	n/a
Time in System	Uncertain	Deterred Disinvestment

foreign subsidiaries' disinvestment produced uncertain results. The Caves and Porter study showed that industry concentration facilitated disinvestment while the asset/sales ratio and time in system were both deterrents.

The difference in the results for industry concentration could have resulted from the use of U.S. industry concentration data to approximate the competitive situations in foreign markets. If foreign markets do not have the same market structure as the U.S., as was assumed in this study, then a source of bias might have been introduced. Caves and Porter used the U.S. industry concentration ratios in conjunction with primarily U.S. businesses, which obviously eliminated this potential bias.

Caves and Porter hypothesized that the assets/sales ratio and time in system variables only became important if the economic analysis justified disinvestment. The assets/sales ratio indicates its relative unattractiveness to a purchaser, while the time in system is an indication of management barriers to disinvestment. As a result of being able to cull the businesses which were not candidates for disinvestment from their data base, Caves' and Porter's study provided better support for their hypotheses.

Another difference in the studies was that Caves and Porter discussed only the disinvesting side. They did not address the issue of who would buy the disinvested businesses. Since the businesses included in their study were primarily large corporations, the potential buyers would probably be the same as postulated by this study, smaller companies with an ability to improve cash flow through cost reductions or sales increases or having access to lower cost funds through government loan guarantees, etc.

The previous major study of foreign disinvestment by Torneden used primarily case studies and interviews with executives in reaching its conclusions.[6] He found that disinvestments were often preceded by top management changes and were influenced by U.S. parent operations. He also stated that most disinvested subsidiaries were not operating in an integrated system.

The statistical analyses of this study confirm his findings concerning integration with strong support of the intrasystem sales variable. It should be noted that his findings were also in opposition to Caves' and Porter's results regarding intrasystem sales.

While not having as strong support statistically, the results for changes in top management and a decrease in system earnings also confirm his results. In addition, the case studies were also supportive of his conclusions.

Thus, this study confirms the findings of Torneden. The results are not as consistent with the Caves and Porter work. Although their conclusions concerning the impact on disinvestment of the number of products produced by a subsidiary were supported, several other variables were neither supported nor opposed. The results for the level of intrasystem sales were the opposite of their conclusions.

The strongest finding of this study in terms of statistical and case study support was the significance of the system ties in deterring disinvestment. The variable which was used as a proxy for interdependence, the level of intrasystem sales, showed strong support for the hypothesis. Another variable which could be considered to be related to the ties with the system, the entry method, showed a lower likelihood of disinvestment for subsidiaries which were newly formed. All other factors being equal, the results showed that subsidiaries more closely tied to the parent were less likely to be disinvested.

Another variable used as a proxy for management barriers, the sales level of the subsidiary, may also have an additional effect. There may be fewer potential purchasers for large subsidiaries. It is likely that subsidiaries would bring higher disinvestment value if sold as going concerns rather than through asset liquidation. Thus, subsidiaries with large sales volume, in addition to being more difficult to disinvest from a managerial standpoint, may also be more difficult to disinvest because of a shortage of potential buyers.

The other contribution of this study has been the consideration of disinvestment in the context of a dynamic process of foreign direct investment. Previous studies have treated disinvestment as an isolated event or phenomenon. This study hypothesized that following the establishment of a subsidiary, changes in industry or competitive conditions could work toward reducing the value of the subsidiary to the parent and increasing its value to a potential buyer. This indicates that disinvestment should be viewed as an extension of the foreign investment process.

III. Areas for Further Research

The primary thrust of this study has been to develop a model of disinvestment activity. This disinvestment model, which hypothesized it to be a function of expected cash flows, discount rates, interdependence, specific assets, and conflicting goals was subjected to several tests. While some of these provided support for the model, others did not. This implies that further studies are warranted.

One of the assumptions made in the testing of the model was that industry concentration ratios in other countries are similar to the U.S. Although a useful working assumption for this study, it is likely that there are differences between countries in the competitive situations for specific industries. Since the hypothesized model relating disinvestment to the competitive situation was not supported, the examination of the role of competition in disinvestment could be undertaken on a more detailed level. Such a study might focus on a specific foreign country and examine the disinvestment of subsidiaries by foreign parents.

Since the results concerning intrasystem sales conflicted with Caves' and

Porter's study, additional work in this area to resolve the conflict would be beneficial.

This study also indicated the existence of conflicting managerial goals as a barrier to disinvestment. Using aggregative data, the importance of these barriers was shown. Since these barriers lead to decisions which are not in the best economic interests of the company, additional study of these barriers is needed.

One method of further examination of the management barriers would be through additional case studies of disinvestment situations. However, this would probably prove to be difficult. As was noted, companies were not cooperative in attempts to discuss disinvestment cases with them. Nevertheless, further attempts along these lines could provide useful information.

Another method of analyzing the role of managerial barriers would be through research into aspects of organizational behavior and psychology. Studies in these disciplines might lead to theories explaining why such barriers might exist and how to deal with them.

Notes

Chapter 1

1. See "The New Data in Annual Reports," *Business Week,* April 24, 1978, p. 129, and William K. Chung, "Sales by Majority-Owned Affiliates of U.S. Companies, 1975," *Survey of Current Business,* February 1977, p. 29.

2. These 180 firms were selected on the basis of appearing on the *Fortune* lists of the 500 largest U.S. industrial firms in 1963 and 1964 and controlling manufacturing subsidiaries in 6 or more foreign countries in 1965 or before. These multinational companies will comprise the sample group for the remainder of the study.

3. Curhan, Joan P., et al., *Tracing the Multinationals* (Cambridge, Mass.: Ballinger Publishing Co.), 1977, p. 19.

4. Harvard Multinational Enterprise Study.

5. Hillman, Richard H. and Soden, John V., "Don't Try to Sell a Pig in a Poke," *Corporate Financing,* November/December, 1971.

6. Wallender, Harvey W., "A Planned Approach to Divestment," *Columbia Journal of World Business,* Spring, 1973, pp. 33-37.

7. Ibid., p. 33.

8. Gilmour, S. Clark, *The Divestment Decision,* unpublished doctoral dissertation, Harvard Business School, 1973.

9. Caves, Richard E. and Porter, Michael E., "Barriers to Exit" in *Essays on Industrial Organization in Honor of Joe S. Bain,* edited by Robert T. Masson and P. David Qualls (Ballinger Publishing Co.: Cambridge, Mass.: Ballinger Publishing Co.)

10. Porter, Michael E., "Please Note the Location of Nearest Exit: Exit Barriers and Planning," *California Management Review,* Winter 1976, pp. 21-33.

11. Hirschman, A. O., "How to Divest in Latin America and Why," *The Multinational Enterprise in Transition,* edited by A. Kapoor and Phillip A. Grub (Princeton, N.J.: The Darwin Press), 1972.

12. Behrman, J. N., "International Divestment: Panacea or Pitfall," *The Multinational Enterprise in Transition,* ibid.

13. Sachdev, Jagdish C., "Disinvestment—Corporate Strategy or Admission of Failure," *Multinational Business,* Dec, 1975. See also: Sachdev, Jadgish C., "Disinvestment: A New

Challenge to Multinationals and a New Threat to Developing Countries," *Multinational Business,* Sept. 1974.

14. Sachdev, Jagdish C., "Disinvestment: A New Problem in Multinational Corporation Host Government Interface," *Management International Review,* Vol. 16, 3/1976, pp. 23-35.

15. Sachdev, "Disinvestment—Corporate Strategy or Admission of Failure."

16. Ibid., p. 16.

17. Ibid., pp. 17-19.

18. Torneden, Roger L., *Foreign Divestment by U.S. Multinational Corporations* (New York: Praeger Publishers), 1975.

19. Boddewyn, J. J., *International Divestment, A Survey of Corporate Experience* (New York: Business International S.A.), 1976.

Chapter 2

1. Hymer, Stephen H., *The International Operations of National Firms: A Study of Direct Foreign Investment* (Cambridge, Mass.: The MIT Press), 1976, p. 33.

2. Ibid, pp. 41-46.

3. Ibid., pp. 37-39.

4. Vernon, Raymond, *Sovereignty at Bay* (New York: Basic Books), 1971.

5. Moxon, Richard W., *Offshore Production in the Less-Developed Countries by American Electronics Companies,* unpublished doctoral thesis, Harvard Business School, 1973.

6. Stobaugh, Robert B., and others, *Nine Investments Abroad and Their Impact at Home,* (Boston, Div. of Res., HBS), 1976.

7. Caves, Richard E., "Causes of Direct Investment: Foreign Firms' Shares in Canadian and U.S. Manufacturing Industries," *The Review of Economics and Statistics,* March 1974, pp. 279-93.

8. Horst, Thomas, "The Industrial Composition of U.S. Exports and Subsidiary Sales to the Canadian Market," *The American Economic Review,* March 1972, pp. 37-45.

9. Aliber, Robert Z., "A Theory of Direct Foreign Investment," in *The Multinational Corporation,* Kindleberger, Charles P. (Cambridge, Mass.: MIT Press), 1970, pp. 17-34.

10. See Lee, C. H., "A Stock Adjustment Analysis of Capital Movements: The United States —Canadian Case," *Journal of Political Economy,* July/August 1969, pp. 512-23; and Rodriguez, Rita M. and Carter, E. Eugene, *International Financial Management* (Englewood Cliffs, N. J.: Prentice-Hall, Inc.), 1976, p. 427.

11. Stobaugh, et al., *Nine Investments Abroad,* p. 213.

12. Vernon, Raymond, "The Location of Economic Activity," *Economic Analysis and the Multinational Enterprise,* edited by John H. Dunning (London: George Allen and Unwin Ltd.), 1974.

13. Stobaugh, Robert B., et al., "U.S. Multinational Enterprises and the U.S. Economy," in Bureau of International Commerce, U.S. Department of Commerce, *The Multinational Corporation,* Vol. 1 (Washington: Superintendent of Documents), 1972, p. 26.

14. Knickerbocker, F.T., *Oligopolistic Reaction and Multinational Enterprise* (Boston: Div. of Research, Grad. School of Bus. Admin., Harvard University), 1973.

15. Graham, Edward M., *Oligopolistic Imitation and European Direct Investment in the United States,* unpublished doctoral thesis, Harvard Business School, 1974.

16. Vernon, Raymond, *Storm Over the Multinationals* (Cambridge, Mass.: Harvard University Press), 1977, pp. 66-69.

Chapter 3

1. Boddewyn, *International Divestment,* pp. 52-53.

2. Porter, "Please Note the Location of Nearest Exit."

3. Gilmour, *The Divestment Decision.*

4. Ibid.

5. Torneden, *Foreign Divestment by U.S. Multinational Corporations.*

6. Ibid.

Chapter 4

1. Curhan, et al., *Tracing the Multinationals.*

2. Robinson, Richard D., *National Control of Foreign Business Entry* (New York: Praeger Publishers), 1976.

3. Franko, Lawrence, *Strategy Choice and Multinational Corporate Tolerance for Joint Ventures with Foreign Partners,* unpublished doctoral thesis, Harvard Business School, 1970; and Stopford, John M. and Wells, Louis T., Jr., *Managing the Multinational Enterprise* (New York: Basic Books), 1972, Chapter 8, 9, and 10.

4. Kitching, John, "Winning and Losing with European Acquisitions," *Harvard Business Review,* March-April 1974, pp. 124-136.

5. Knickerbocker, Frederick T., *Market Structure and Market Power Consequences of Foreign Direct Investment by Multinational Corporations* (Washington, D.C.: Center for

Multinational Studies), 1976. See also Rose, Sanford, "Why the Multinational Tide is Ebbing," *Fortune,* August 1977, pp. 111-20.

6. Vaupel, J. W. and Curhan, J. P., *The World's Multinational Enterprises* (Cambridge, Mass.: Division of Research, Harvard Business School), 1973.

7. "Concentration Ratios in Manufacturing," *1972 Census of Manufactures* (United States Department of Commerce), 1975.

8. Knickerbocker, *Oligopolistic Reaction and Multinational Enterprise,* pp. 221-22.

9. Robbins, Sidney M., and Stobaugh, Robert B., *Money in the Multinational Enterprise* (New York: Basic Books, Inc.), 1973, pp. 193-99. A further explanation is attached as Appendix.

10. The probability of the sign is shown in parentheses. The program assumes the data are a sample from a population and computes a distribution for the estimates of the coefficients. Taking this distribution, the program indicates the percentage which have the same sign as the mean estimate. See Appendix.

Chapter 5

1. Gilmour, *The Disinvestment Decision,* and Torneden, *Foreign Divestment by U.S. Multinational Corporations.*

Chapter 7

1. Caves and Porter, "Barriers to Exit," and Porter, "Please Note Location of Nearest Exit."

2. Porter, "Please Note Location of Nearest Exit," p. 29.

3. Ibid., pp. 30-33.

4. Caves and Porter used the percentage of shipments accounted for by the four largest firms in the industry.

5. Caves and Porter used a measure of overall company diversity which included the number of different SIC codes.

6. Torneden, *Foreign Divestment by U.S. Multinational Corporations.*

Appendix A

The Logistic Regression Model

As the logistic regression model has not been frequently used in business applications, it may bear additional explanation. (See Robbins and Stobaugh, *Money and the Multinational Enterprise*.) As noted in Chapter 4, the general formulation of the model is:

$$\log e \; \frac{p}{1-p} \; = \; \beta_0 + \beta_1 X_1 + \beta_2 X_2 + \beta_n X_n$$

where:

p = "true" but uncertain long run fraction of subsidiaries which will be disinvested.

X_n = a variable which is hypothesized to be related to disinvestment.

For each variable, the logistic regression model fits an s-shaped curve, a logistic curve, to the data. Since the dependent variable is the probability that a firm will or will not be disinvested, the value of the variable cannot be greater than one or less than zero. This results in a curve shaped as follows:

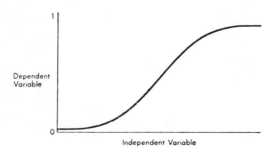

The obvious major difference in this analysis as compared to standard regression models is that it does not assume a linear relationship. With the linear models, using a least squares approach a straight line would be fitted so that it passed through or came close to 0 or 1. This would allow predicted values of the dependent variable to exceed this range and have a negative value or a value greater than 1. Such results do not make sense when the dependent variable is of an either-or nature such as this case. The logistic regression model eliminates this problem by fitting a logistic curve such that at the extremes of the independent variable the value of the dependent variable approaches 0 or 1.

For this study, the important consideration was the impact of the variables on the probability of disinvestment. The purpose of the study was not to examine the absolute value of the coefficients but rather only to determine whether the coefficients had the hypothesized positive or negative effect on disinvestment. Thus, the key element for this study was the sign of the coefficient.

To determine a level of confidence in the sign of the coefficient, a probability of sign for the estimate of the coefficient was given. This calculation was based on the assumption that the data used in the test was a sample of a larger population of data. Thus, the coefficient for a variable which was given was the mean estimate of a range of coefficients which could be generated by the larger population. A distribution of these possible coefficients was calculated with an assumed normal distribution pattern. Given this distribution, the probability of sign indicates the percentage of the distribution of coefficient estimates which has the same sign as the mean estimate.

Thus, even though the estimate may not have been the "true" coefficient for the larger sample, the probability of sign provided a level of certainty about the sign of the "true" coefficient. A probability of sign of 1.0 would indicate that the entire distribution of coefficients had the same sign as the mean estimate. A probability of sign of .5 indicates that 50% of the distribution had the same sign as the mean, while 50% did not. (A probability of sign of .5 would also mean that the mean estimate of the coefficient was 0.) A probability of sign of .9 would therefore indicate a 90% certainty that the sign of the "true" coefficient would have the same sign as the mean estimate.

Bibliography

Aliber, Robert A., "A Theory of Direct Foreign Investment," in *The Multinational Corporation,* Kindleberger, Charles P. (Cambridge, Mass.: MIT Press), 1970, pp. 17-34.

Behrman, J.N., "International Divestment: Panacea or Pitfall," *The Multinational Enterprise in Transition,* edited by A. Kapoor and Phillip A. Grub (Princeton, N.J.: The Darwin Press), 1972.

Boddewyn, J.J., *International Divestment, A Survey of Corporate Experience* (New York: Business International S.A.), 1976, pp. 52-53.

Business Week, April 24, 1978, p. 129.

Caves, Richard E., "Causes of Direct Investment: Foreign Firms' Shares in Canadian and U.S. Manufacturing Industries," *The Review of Economics and Statistics,* March 1974, pp. 279-93.

————, and Porter, Michael E., "Barriers to Exit," in *Essays on Industrial Organization in Honor of Joe S. Bain,* edited by Masson, Robert T. and Qualls, P. David (Cambridge: Ballinger Publishing Co.)

Chung, William K., "Sales by Majority-Owned Affiliates of U.S. Companies, 1975," *Survey of Current Business,* February 1977, p. 29.

"Concentration Ratios in Manufacturing," *1972 Census of Manufactures* (United States Department of Commerce), 1975.

Curhan, Joan P., et al., *Tracing the Multinationals* (Cambridge, Mass.: Ballinger Publishing Co.), 1977, p. 19.

Franko, Lawrence, *Strategy Choice and Multinational Corporate Tolerance for Joint Ventures with Foreign Partners,* unpublished doctoral thesis, Harvard Business School, 1970.

Gilmour, S. Clark, *The Divestment Decision,* unpublished doctoral thesis, Harvard Business School, 1973.

Graham, Edward M., *Oligopolistic Imitation and European Direct Investment in the United States,* unpublished doctoral thesis, Harvard Business School, 1974.

Gruber, William H., et al., "The R&D Factor in International Trade and International Investment of United States Industries" in Wells, Louis T., Jr. et al., *The Product Life Cycle and International Trade* (Boston, Mass.: Division of Research, Harvard Business School), 1972.

Hillman, Richard H. and Soden, John V., "Don't Try to Sell a Pig in a Poke," *Corporate Financing,* November/December, 1971.

Hirschman, A.O., "How to Divest in Latin America and Why," *The Multinational Enterprise in Transition,* edited by A. Kapoor and Phillip A. Grub (Princeton, N.J.: The Darwin Press), 1972.

Horst, Thomas, *American Exports and Foreign Direct Investments,* Discussion Paper No. 362 (Harvard Institute of Economic Research, Cambridge), May 1974.

————. "The Industrial Composition of U.S. Exports and Subsidiary Sales to the Canadian Market," *The American Economic Review,* March 1972, pp. 37-45.

Hymer, Stephen H., *The International Operations of National Firms: A Study of Direct Foreign Investment* (Cambridge, Mass.: The MIT Press), 1976, p. 33.

Kitching, John, "Winning and Losing with European Acquisitions," *Harvard Business Review,* March-April 1974, pp. 124-36.

Knickerbocker, Frederick T., *Market Structure and Market Power Consequences of Foreign Direct Investment by Multinational Corporations* (Washington, D.C.: Center for Multinational Studies), 1976.

————. *Oligopolistic Reaction and Multinational Enterprise* (Boston: Div. of Research, Grad. School of Bus. Admin., Harvard University), 1973.

Lee, C.H., "A Stock Adjustment Analysis of Capital Movements: The United States—Canadian Case," *Journal of Political Economy,* July/August 1969, pp. 512-23.

Moxon, Richard W., *Offshore Production in the Less-Developed Countries by American Electronics Companies,* unpublished doctoral thesis, Harvard Business School, 1973.

Porter, Michael E., "Please Note Location of Nearest Exit: Exit Barriers and Planning," *California Management Review,* Winter 1976, p. 21-33.

Robbins, Sidney M. and Stobaugh, Robert B., *Money in the Multinational Enterprise* (New York: Basic Books, Inc.), 1973.

Robinson, Richard D., *National Control of Foreign Business Entry* (New York: Praeger Publishers), 1976.

Rodriguez, Rita M. and Carter, E. Eugene, *International Financial Management* (Englewood Cliffs, N.J.: Prentice-Hall, Inc.), 1976, p. 427.

Roemer, John E., *U.S.-Japanese Competition in International Markets* (Institute of International Studies, University of California, Berkeley), 1975.

Rose, Sanford, "Why the Multinational Tide is Ebbing," *Fortune,* August 1977, pp. 111-20.

Sachdev, Jagdish C., "Disinvestment—Corporate Strategy or Admission of Failure," *Multinational Business,* December 1975.

_____. "Disinvestment: A New Challenge to Multinationals and a New Threat to Developing Countries," *Multinational Business,* September 1974.

_____. "Disinvestment: A New Problem in Multinational Corporation Host Government Interface," *Management International Review,* Vol. 16, 3/1976, pp. 23-35.

Stobaugh, Robert B. and others, *Nine Investments Abroad and Their Impact at Home* (Boston, Div. of Res., HBS), 1976.

_____, et al., "U.S. Multinational Enterprises and the U.S. Economy," in Bureau of International Commerce, U.S. Department of Commerce, *The Multinational Corporation,* Vol. 1 (Washington: Superintendent of Documents), 1972, p. 26.

_____. "Utilizing Technical Know-How in a Foreign Investment and Licensing Program," Harvard Business School, 9-371-321.

Stopford, John M. and Wells, Louis T., Jr., *Managing the Multinational Enterprise* (New York: Basic Books), 1972, Chapters 8, 9, and 10.

Torneden, Robert L., *Foreign Divestment by U.S. Multinational Corporations* (New York: Praeger Publishers), 1975.

Vaupel, J.W., and Curhan, J.P., *The World's Multinational Enterprises* (Cambridge, Mass.: Division of Research, Harvard Business School), 1973.

Vernon, Raymond, "The Location of Economic Activity," *Economic Analysis and the Multinational Enterprise,* edited by John H. Dunning (London: George Allen and Unwin Ltd.), 1974.

_____. *Sovereignty at Bay* (New York: Basic Books), 1971.

_____. *Storm Over the Multinationals* (Cambridge, Mass.: Harvard University Press), 1977, pp. 66-69.

Wallender, Harvey W., "A Planned Approach to Divestment," *Columbia Journal of World Business,* Spring, 1973, pp. 33-37.

Index

ACC, 66-68, 69-70
Acquired subsidiaries, 27, 39-40
Aliber, Robert Z., 15
AMI, 63, 65-68
American Machinery, Inc., 63, 65-68
American Standard, 63-65, 69-70
Assets, 8, 15, 25. *See also* Specific assets
Assets/sales, 39, 42-43, 45-46, 70, 72-73, 75-76
Australian Climax Commercial, 66-68, 69-70
Australian Climax Ltd., 65-68

Bamberger Industrial Equipment, 67-68, 70
Behrman, J. N., 9
Boddewyn, J. J., 11, 23
Book loss, 26
Book value, 26, 68
Brand names. *See* Trademarks

Cannon, Ltd., 66-68
Capital, alternative uses of, 18, 29
Capital intensive, 39, 42, 64
Capital markets, 15, 28
Capital needs, 50
Cash flow, 21-24, 26, 28-30, 33, 35-36, 69, 71-72; method, 30; present value of, 21-23, 24-25, 28-29, 71; relevant, 24-25, 29, 38, 71
Caves, Richard E., 8, 15, 30, 73-77, 78
CEO. *See* Chief Executive Officer
Chief Executive Officer, 52, 53, 61-62, 73
Chief Operating Officer, 52, 53, 57, 61-62, 73
Collusion, 14
Commercial Products, 66
Commodity product, 16
Competitive advantage, 13-18, 23-25, 29, 36, 71; in capital markets, 15
Competition: in host market, 14-15, 17, 35-37; price, 15

Conflicting management goals, 9, 27, 28-29, 33, 43-44, 49, 70, 72-73, 79
COO. *See* Chief Operating Officer
Cost of Capital, 15, 22, 71; *See also* Discount rate

Data: cross-sectional, 35-36; external, 39, 61; missing, 40
Depreciation, 22
Differentiated product, 13
Discount rate, 22, 24, 28-29, 33, 36, 69, 71-72; for local firm, 23-24
Disinvestment: analysis, 27; barriers to, 27, 50, 61, 71, 79; case studies of, 7, 10-11; decisions, 27, 30, 39, 61, 63; economically justified, 9, 22, 26-27, 37, 39, 49, 61, 71; facilitators of, 49, 51-53, 57, 61; gap, 10; models, 8, 28-30, 32-33, 36, 49, 69-70; partial, 34; planned, 7, 9; policy, 9-10; probability (likelihood) of, 17-18, 28-29, 33, 35, 36-38, 40-45, 57, 71, 72, 75, 78, 85-86; process of, 7-8; product, 34, 37, 41; stimuli, 62, 72-73; strategy, 7; studies of, 2, 9; value, 22, 25-29, 71; voluntary, 33
Durable and specific assets. *See* Specific assets

Earnings: decrease in system, 28, 50, 52-54, 57, 61, 62, 70, 73; of a company, 49-50; per share, 26, 52
Economic variables, 17, 26, 71
Economies of scale, 13, 15, 22
Electronic companies, U.S., 14-15
Entry year, 44, 45-46
Error corrections, 1, 35
Exchange of threat strategy, 17
Exchange rate, 22
Exit: barriers to, 8-9, 35, 75 *(See also* Disinvestment, barriers to); rate, 2

Exporting, 14
Expropriation, 2, 33
External factors, 18, 24, 38
Extractive subsidiaries, 13, 34

Firms, largest in industry, 37
Follow-the-leader strategy, 17, 18
Forced sales, 33
Foreign direct investment: active, 16-17, 18, 23, 24, 30, 71; dynamic models, 14-17; reactive, 17-19, 24, 25, 30, 71; theories of, 13
Fortune 500 companies, 1, 10, 33

Gilmour, S. Clark, 7, 27
Goals, of managers, 26
Graham, Edward M., 17

Harvard Multinational Enterprise Study, 1, 11, 33, 36, 51, 62, 72
Heating business, 63-64
Heavy machinery, 66
Hillman, Richard H., 7
Hirschman, A. O., 9
Host government, 22
Horst, Thomas, 15
Hymer, Stephen H., 13, 14

Ideal Standard France, 64-65, 70
Identification with subsidiaries, 27, 39, 44
Industry: concentration, 37, 41, 45-46, 72-73, 75-76, 78; stability, 30, (See also Oligopoly); U.S., 37
Information-related barriers, 9
Innovation, 14
Interdependence, 28-29, 33, 38, 42, 69, 72-73, 75
Intrasystem sales, 38, 42, 45-46, 72-73, 75, 77-78
Investment, 15, 22

Joint production assets, 8, 9
Joint ventures, 34, 63

Knickerbocker, Frederick T., 17, 35

Labor intensive products, 64
Length of time in system, 27, 39-40, 75-76

Likelihood of disinvestment. See Disinvestment, probability of
Linear regression, 85
Listening post strategy, 17, 18
Local firm, 13, 23, 36; competitive advantages of, 23; ownership of, 23
Logistic regression, 40, 53, 62, 73, 85-86
Longitudinal model, 35-36

Majority owned subsidiaries, 34
Management: abilities of, 15, 23; barriers, 9, 39, 49, 79; behavior of, 8; change in, 11, 27, 30, 50, 52-53, 57, 61, 70, 77; failure, 7, 8, 9, 26-27, 29, 70; perceptions of, 25
Manchester, University of, 10
Manufacturing subsidiaries, 13, 34; growth in, 2
Market: competition, 29; instability in, 36, (See also Oligopoly); stability in, 18
Marketing abilities, 13, 16
Maximize: failure to, net present value, 26, 30, 39; growth, 26
Method of entry, 39-40, 43, 45-46, 72-73, 78
Mining subsidiaries, 34
Moxon, Richard W., 14
Multinational companies, 1, 35; British, 10; non-U.S. based, 36; U.S., 33, 36
Multiple regression, 45, 61

Nationalization, 2, 33
Net income, 52, 57
Newly formed subsidiaries, 27, 39-40, 43

Oligopoly, 13, 15, 17-18, 24, 25, 30
Opportunity rate, 18, 29
Overhead costs, 25

Parent company profits, 28, 30
PIMS Program, 73
Porter, Michael E., 8, 9, 30, 73-77, 79
Portfolio theory, 16
Present value model, 21, 25. See also Cash flow, present value of
Probability of disinvestment. See Disinvestment, probability of
Probability of sign, 40-45, 53-61, 86
Product life cycle model, 14, 17, 35
Products, number produced, 37, 41, 45-46, 72-73, 77

Profit maximization strategy, 17-18
Production, 13, 15
Proxy (surrogate) variable, 36, 37, 46
Purchase price, 26, 38

Return: on investment, 11, 18, 50; on sales, 50
Risk: individual, 26-27; minimization strategy, 17-18, 39; perceptions of, 17, 18, 19, 30; political, 24
Robbins, Sidney M., 85
Robinson, Richard D., 33

Sachdev, Jagdish C., 10
Sales subsidiaries, 34
Sales within system. *See* Intrasystem sales
Service subsidiaries, 34
Sharing of production factors, 24, 69
SIC code, 37, 41
Soden, John V., 7
Social problems, 27
Specific assets, 8, 25, 28-29, 33, 38, 39, 42, 69-70, 72-73
Standard Industrial Classification code, 37, 41

Stobaugh, Robert B., 15, 16, 85
Stock price, 49-50
Strategic Planning Institute, 73
Subsidiaries: expected profitability, 21; growth, 2; poorly performing, 10, 27-28, 29, 35, 49-50, 75; sales of, 40, 43-44, 45-46, 72-73, 78; size of, 27, 39-40; valuation of, 29

Tariffs, 14, 15
Tax shelters, 34
Technology, 16, 21-22
Textile machinery, 66-68
Time lag, 50, 52, 53, 57, 61
Trade, 15
Trademarks (Brand names), 8, 15, 25, 69-70
Torneden, Robert L., 10, 11, 27, 28, 77
Turn around situations, 9, 29

Vernon, Raymond, 14, 15, 16

Wallender, Harvey W., 7